James Joyce

James Joyce

By A. WALTON LITZ

Princeton University

TWAYNE PUBLISHERS

A DIVISION OF G. K. HALL & CO., BOSTON

ISBN 0-8057-1300-X

Contents

Preface

Anyone who decides to write a general study of Joyce's art is confronted with two formidable problems: the complexity of the works themselves, and the size of the critical literature which has accumulated around them. To the average reader, Joyce's works —especially *Ulysses* and *Finnegans Wake*—have become frightening symbols of the difficulty of modern literature; they seem to cry out for explication and commentary, and this cry has not gone unanswered. Over the past two decades the scholarly "Joyce factory" has produced a vast number of specialized studies, until even the accomplished reader hesitates to explore such controversial areas as Joyce's relationship to Aquinas, or his methods of composition, where the signs clearly warn: "Keep out! Specialists only." Most of these limited studies have been necessary—Joyce, not the scholars, created the demand for them—but we are always in danger of exchanging Joyce's art for what one critic has called "a textbook ideogram of his works."

In the present study I have tried to avoid specialized debates and minor critical controversies; the reader who wishes to pursue these will find that I have provided him with a starting point in the Notes and References and in the Selective Bibliography. I have also tried to avoid overly detailed analysis of particular passages, although in the case of Joyce's most difficult works one can hardly discuss the general significance of a passage without first clarifying the local problems. Biographical material has been supplied only where it is of critical importance. My aim has been to give a coherent account of Joyce's artistic development, indicating some of the major approaches to each work. It is my hope that the reader will find this book most valuable for its general point of view.

The study of Joyce's work is, of necessity, a cooperative enterprise, and I am deeply indebted to a number of other critics. My particular debts are acknowledged in the footnotes; larger obligations are indicated by the Selective Bibliography, which draws together the books and articles I have found most illuminating. I would like to acknowledge my special debt to Professor Richard Ellmann, whose *James Joyce* supplied me with most of the biographical information used in this study.

Page references for Joyce's major works have been inserted directly into the text in parentheses. I have used the Modern Library edition of *Ulysses*, and the Viking Press edition of *Finnegans Wake* (which has the same pagination as the Faber & Faber edition). In citing *Ulysses* I have given two page references: the first reference applies to the 1934 edition, the second to the 1961 edition. All other page references in the text are to *The Portable James Joyce*, edited by Harry Levin (The Viking Press), which contains *Dubliners, A Portrait of the Artist as a Young Man, Exiles,* and the *Collected Poems*.

I am grateful to the Viking Press for permission to quote from *Dubliners, A Portrait of the Artist as a Young Man, Exiles, Finnegans Wake,* the *Collected Poems,* the *Critical Writings of James Joyce,* and *Letters of James Joyce.* I am grateful to Random House for permission to quote from *Ulysses,* and to New Directions for permission to quote from *Stephen Hero.*

A. Walton Litz

Princeton University
August 20, 1965

The publication of this study in paperback has given me the opportunity to make a few changes in the text and notes, and to revise completely the Selected Bibliography.

A. W. L.
April 24, 1972

Chronology

1882 James Joyce born in Dublin on February 2, the eldest son of John Stanislaus Joyce, an improvident tax collector, and Mary Jane Joyce.

1884 Birth of Stanislaus Joyce. Of the ten Joyce children who survived infancy, Stanislaus was closest to James.

1888 In September Joyce entered Clongowes Wood College, a Jesuit boarding school; there he remained (except for holidays) until June 1891.

1891 A crucial year in Joyce's life. Financial difficulties forced John Joyce to withdraw James from Clongowes Wood in June. The death of Parnell on October 6 deeply affected the nine-year-old boy, who wrote a poem, "Et Tu, Healy," denouncing Parnell's "betrayer," Tim Healy; John Joyce was so pleased that he had the poem printed, but no copy has survived. Christmas dinner in the Joyce household was marred by a violent scene later described in *Portrait of the Artist*.

1893 In April Joyce entered another Jesuit school, Belvedere College, where he remained until 1898, making a brilliant academic record.

1898 Joyce began to attend University College, Dublin, a Jesuit institution founded by Cardinal Newman. While there, his revolt against Catholicism and provincial patriotism took form.

1899 In May Joyce opposed his fellow students and refused to sign a letter attacking the "heresy" of Yeats's *Countess Cathleen*.

1900 A year of literary activity. In January Joyce read a paper on "Drama and Life" before the college literary society (see *Stephen Hero*); in April his essay on "Ibsen's New Drama" appeared in the distinguished *Fortnightly Review*.

1901 Late in the year Joyce published "The Day of the Rabblement," an essay attacking the provincialism of the Irish theater (originally designed for a college magazine, it was rejected by the Jesuit adviser).

1902 In February Joyce read a paper on the Irish poet James Clarence Mangan, claiming that Mangan had been the victim of narrow nationalism.

Joyce, who received his degree in October, finally decided to study medicine in Paris. He left Dublin in the late autumn, pausing briefly in London to visit Yeats and to investigate possible outlets for his writing.

1903 Once in Paris, Joyce soon lost interest in medicine and began to write reviews for a Dublin newspaper. On April 10 he received a telegram, "MOTHER DYING COME HOME FATHER," and immediately returned to Dublin. His mother died on August 13.

1904 Early in 1904 Joyce began work on his autobiographical novel with a short piece called "A Portrait of the Artist": this was later expanded into *Stephen Hero* and then recast to make *A Portrait of the Artist as a Young Man*.

The situation of the Joyce family had worsened after Mary Joyce's death, and James gradually withdrew from the family. In March he took a job as teacher in a Dalkey school, remaining there until the end of June. On June 10 Joyce met Nora Barnacle and soon fell in love with her. Since he was opposed to marriage as an institution, and could not live with Nora in Dublin, Joyce decided to make his way in Europe. He and Nora left Dublin on October 8, traveling through London and Zurich to Pola, where Joyce began teaching English at the Berlitz School.

1905 Joyce moved to Trieste in March, and a son, Giorgio, was born on July 27. Three months later Joyce's younger brother, Stanislaus, joined him in Trieste. Late in the year Joyce submitted the manuscript of *Dubliners* to a publisher, but it was not until 1914—after years of controversy —that the book appeared.

1906 In July 1906 Joyce moved to Rome, where he worked in a
1907 bank until March of the next year; he then returned to Trieste and resumed his language teaching. In May a Lon-

don publisher issued *Chamber Music*. A daughter, Lucia Anna, was born on July 26.

In September Joyce began revising *Stephen Hero* and con-
1908   tinued this work into the next year, but after finishing three chapters he temporarily abandoned the manuscript.

1909   On August 1 Joyce traveled to Ireland for a visit. The next month he came back to Trieste, gained financial support, and returned to Dublin where he opened a cinema.

1910   Joyce returned to Trieste in January, and the cinema venture soon collapsed. During his first visit to Dublin, Joyce underwent an emotional crisis later transformed into the substance of his play, *Exiles*.

1911   During these years the controversy over *Dubliners* became
1912   an obsession with Joyce. Finally, in July, 1912, he made his last trip to Dublin, but was unable to arrange for publication. Joyce left Dublin in great bitterness, and on the return journey to Trieste wrote a savage broadside, *Gas from a Burner*.

1913   Late in the year Joyce began to correspond with Ezra Pound; his luck was changing.

1914   Joyce's *annus mirabilis*. Serial publication of *A Portrait of the Artist as a Young Man* began in the *Egoist* (instalments ran from February, 1914 to September, 1915). *Dubliners* was finally published in June. In March Joyce began drafting *Ulysses;* but he soon suspended work on the novel to write *Exiles*.

1915   *Exiles* was completed in the spring. In spite of the war Joyce was allowed to depart in June for neutral Switzerland.

1916   *Portrait* was published in book form on December 29.

1917   During this year Joyce underwent his first eye operation. By the end of 1917 Joyce had finished drafting the first three episodes of *Ulysses;* the structure of the novel was already taking shape.

1918   In March the *Little Review* (New York) began to serialize *Ulysses. Exiles* was published on May 25.

1919   In October Joyce returned to Trieste, where he taught English and drove *Ulysses* toward completion.

1920   At the insistence of Ezra Pound, Joyce moved to Paris in early July. In October a complaint from the Society for the Suppression of Vice stopped publication of *Ulysses* in the *Little Review* (the opening pages of "Oxen of the Sun" were the last to appear).

1921 This year was devoted to completing the last episodes of *Ulysses* and to revising the entire work.

1922 *Ulysses* was published on February 2, Joyce's fortieth birthday.

1923 On March 10 Joyce wrote the first pages of *Finnegans Wake* (known before publication in 1939 as *Work in Progress*). He had been actively planning for this new work through several years.

1924 The first published fragment of *Finnegans Wake* appeared in April. During the next fourteen years Joyce was to publish most of *Finnegans Wake* in preliminary versions.

1927- Between April, 1927, and November, 1929, Joyce pub-
1929 lished early versions of *Finnegans Wake*, Parts I and III, in the experimental magazine *transition*. *Anna Livia Plurabelle* (FW I. viii) was published in book form on October 20, 1928. During the next ten years several sections of *Work in Progress* were published as books (see Bibliography).

1931 In May the Joyces traveled to London, and on July 4 James and Nora Joyce were married at a registry office ("for testamentary reasons"). Joyce's father died on December 29;

1932 and a grandson, Stephen Joyce, was born on February 15 of the next year. Both events affected Joyce profoundly: see his poem written at the time, "Ecce Puer." In March Joyce's daughter, Lucia, suffered a nervous breakdown; she never recovered, and the remainder of Joyce's life was darkened by this event.

1933 Late in the year an American court ruled that *Ulysses* was not pornographic; this famous decision led to the first authorized American publication of the work in February of the next year (the first English edition was issued in 1936).

1934 Most of this year was spent in Switzerland, so that Joyce could be near Lucia (who was confined to an institution near Zurich) and could consult a Zurich doctor who had cared for his failing eyesight since 1930.

1935- During these years Joyce labored slowly to complete *Fin-*

1938   *negans Wake;* residence in Paris was broken by frequent trips through France, Switzerland, and Denmark.

1939   *Finnegans Wake* was published on May 4, but Joyce received a copy in time for his fifty-seventh birthday.

1940   After the fall of France, the Joyces managed to reach Zu-
1941   rich; James Joyce died there on January 13, 1941, after an abdominal operation.

CHAPTER 1

A Life of Allegory

> . . . every honest to goodness man in the land of the space of today
> knows that his back life will not stand being written about in black
> and white. Putting truth and untruth together a shot may be made at
> what this hybrid actually was like to look at.
>
> —*Finnegans Wake* (169)

K EATS once said that "a Man's life of any worth is a continual allegory—and very few eyes can see the Mystery of his life —a life like the scriptures, figurative . . . Shakespeare led a life of Allegory; his works are the comments on it." [1] Behind this characteristic declaration lies one of the oldest of critical assumptions: the belief that a work of art is an extension of its creator's personality, that the life can be understood through the work and the work through the life. The mind of the artist is the most obvious, and most intriguing, source of his work's form, and we cannot rightfully ignore it, even if our curiosity would allow us to do so. The basic question in biographical criticism is not "should it exist?" but "how should it be conducted?" Each literary movement carries with it a special view of the relationship between an artist's life and his work. The Neo-Classical critics were interested in biography as a revelation of "universal" qualities; since the function of art was conceived as an imitation of general nature, biographical criticism was focused on those aspects of the writer's life which were held in common with other men. Dr. Johnson's *Lives of the Poets* reflected this interest in general human nature, but these biographies also revealed a new concern with the particular circumstances of the writer, those qualities which separate him from other men; already the Romantic complications of the biographical problem were at hand.

The Romantic interest in confession and self-revelation made biographical criticism both more important and more difficult. When the imaginative process is turned inward, and the artist's ego becomes his subject, new problems of interpretation are forced upon us. The Neo-Classical interest in general nature, combined with the lack of biographical information on many early authors, had tended to restrain biographical speculation; but the self-revelations of the great Romantic writers soon led to new critical methods and to the careful preservation of biographical materials (both by the writer and by his admirers). This emphasis on biographical patterns and the creative process was, of course, intensified by the discoveries of modern psychology and psychoanalysis.

In our time the trend of critical theory has been toward a more and more cautious treatment of biographical materials,[2] and to the extent that this trend is a reaction against the naïve methods of earlier generations it is a healthy sign. However, modern theorists have been more successful in pointing out the dangers of crude biographical criticism than in devising more sophisticated approaches to the problem. Our criteria when using biographical information must still be, in large measure, pragmatic ones; and this pragmatism is put to a severe test in the case of Joyce's works, where an obvious and sustained use of autobiographical experiences is combined with extreme subtlety—not to say ambiguity—in treatment. In his Preface to *My Brother's Keeper*, an account of Joyce's early years by his brother Stanislaus, T. S. Eliot makes a distinction between two types of writers on the basis of how they exploit personal experience. Writers of the first type, such as Shakespeare, have transformed their experiences into something so objective—so "figurative," to use Keats's term—that the connections between personality and art are beyond our reach:

It is difficult to believe that greater knowledge about the private life of Shakespeare could much modify our judgment or enhance our enjoyment of his plays; no theory about the origin or mode of composition of the Homeric poems could alter our appreciation of them as poetry. With a writer like Goethe, on the other hand, our interest in the man is inseparable from our interest in the work; and we are impelled to supplement and correct what he tells us in various ways about himself, with information from outside sources; the more we know about the man, the better, we think, we may come to understand his poetry and his prose.[3]

Joyce obviously belongs with Goethe in this grouping of writers, but we will do well to remember that, even in the most straightforward autobiography, personal experience has been transformed by conventions and circumstance; the act of writing is itself an experience that changes the author's personality. And if this is true of the simplest attempts at self-examination, how much more relevant it is to Joyce's complex works, in which we are confronted with infinitely more subtle transformations. The autobiographical figures in Joyce's fiction—from the Stephen of *Stephen Hero* to Shem the Penman in *Finnegans Wake*—must be taken as *personae:* as masks through which the author speaks, masks which often conceal more than they reveal. Even in the early *Stephen Hero* the conventions of the novel have worked changes on Joyce's personality, and by the time we reach *Finnegans Wake* we are faced with a grotesque autobiographical figure who can best be viewed as an embodiment of the sterile qualities in Joyce's life; Shem is really a burlesque of the earlier *personae.*

As if the theoretical problems raised by Joyce's use of biographical materials were not enough, the facts of his life have long been obscured by the "unfacts" of rumor, legend, and deliberate distortion. Joyce's authorized biographer of the 1930's, Herbert Gorman, actually wrote a biography of Stephen Dedalus; Gorman mingled biographical facts with fictional attitudes, and Joyce—who carefully aided and hindered Gorman—was an active party to this distortion.[4] At one point in *Finnegans Wake* the medieval Irish *Martyrology of O'Gorman* is rendered as *"the Martyrology of Gorman"* (349.24), and this is a fair description of Gorman's study.[5] Joyce seems to have deliberately made the "authorized" biography a part of the artistic process which simultaneously revealed and concealed his inner life.

In recent years careful research and a better understanding of Joyce's artistic techniques have led to more objective biography. Richard Ellmann's monumental *James Joyce* and Kevin Sullivan's more limited *Joyce among the Jesuits* have provided a foundation for responsible biographical criticism. Throughout this study I have drawn from these works, or referred to them, wherever a knowledge of Joyce's life seems to have critical relevance, but the early years of his life demand more systematic treatment. For it was during these years that the basic rhythms of his personality and art were established. This statement does not mean, as some critics have claimed, that Joyce ceased to assimilate new experiences after he left Dublin. In spite of his self-imposed exile,

his failing sight, and the solipsism of his last years, Joyce continued to expand his subject matter. But it is true that Joyce's works
always lead us back to the youthful experiences that became
archetypes in his imagination. In this opening chapter I shall deal
only with the first twenty years of Joyce's life, the years before his
first departure for Paris in December, 1902. These are the years
revisited in *A Portrait of the Artist as a Young Man,* and I hope
my treatment of them will disabuse the reader of any notion that
the *Portrait* is straightforward autobiography. I have not attempted a connected account of Joyce's early life—for that story
one must go to Richard Ellmann's opening chapters; instead, I
have concentrated upon those personal relationships and patterns
of behavior which help us to understand the themes and struc-
tures of all his works.

I *Home*

Near the end of *A Portrait of the Artist as a Young Man* Ste-
phen Dedalus tells his companion Cranly of his decision to leave
Ireland, and Cranly subjects Stephen to some probing questions.
Finally Stephen turns upon his companion and says:

—Look here, Cranly . . . You have asked me what I would do
and what I would not do. I will tell you what I will do and what I
will not do. I will not serve that in which I no longer believe, whether
it call itself my home, my fatherland, or my church: and I will try to
express myself in some mode of life or art as freely as I can and as
wholly as I can, using for my defence the only arms I allow myself
to use—silence, exile, and cunning. (518)

The whole weight of the novel bears down on this self-conscious
statement of belief, which sums up the objects of Stephen's revolt
and the nature of his resolution; and it was with this declaration
in mind that I divided the present chapter into brief surveys of
the young Joyce's responses to home, fatherland, and church.

In *A Portrait of the Artist* Stephen visualizes his escape from
Ireland as a flight to freedom. Like his fabulous namesake, Daedalus, he will escape the island which imprisons him, fly past the
nets set to trap him. The first of these nets, in Stephen's mind, is
his family; and when we look at Joyce's early life we find that his
relationships with his mother and father, like those of Stephen,
reflected in miniature his responses to the demands of Irish life.

His father embodied many of the attractive but self-defeating qualities of Irish nationalism, and his mother was a model of devout but uncritical Catholicism. Thus, in the first experiences of childhood, Joyce encountered the two forces which dominated Irish life; and his later struggle to escape these forces was inevitably a struggle against home as well as against nation and church.

However, it would be a mistake to take Joyce's fiction as a guide and to think of him as a sullen rebel against parental authority. Although he was often embarrassed by his father, whose main interest lay in "jollification," Joyce was genuinely fond of him and shared his interest in the complex public life of Dublin. There was never an easy relationship between father and son— John Stanislaus Joyce grew more irascible and violent as his fortunes declined—but James never shared the cold hatred that his brother Stanislaus felt for their father. Toward his mother, too, Joyce was usually considerate and often tender. Stephen Dedalus' refusal of his mother's dying request that he kneel and pray for her, referred to early in *Ulysses* (10, 8), is a dramatic distortion of a complex human relationship.[6] Joyce's letters to his mother written during his first visits to Paris reveal the depth of his affection and also the extent to which he depended upon her.

Although Catholicism and Irish nationalism were constant companions in the Joyce household, it may have been the declining family fortune which had the greatest impact on James. The inefficiency of Joyce's father and his wasteful habits gradually undermined family finances and family solidarity. When James entered the fashionable Clongowes Wood College in 1888, his family was quite well-to-do; by the time he had reached Belvedere College, five years later, his father had been dismissed from the Rates office on a small pension. The family had now begun a long series of removals to cheaper dwellings; the next few years reduced them to near-poverty. This steady decline in the family's financial and social status contributed to the feelings of alienation and isolation which marked Joyce's adolescent personality. As he grew toward maturity Joyce maintained much of his affection for his parents, but he could no longer accept their worlds as his. The home which had seemed a secure refuge to the child became a drab, stultifying, lower-middle-class environment from which he had to escape. This gradual alienation from his home paralleled

Joyce's movements away from unquestioning faith in church and fatherland, and also helped to accelerate them.

II *Fatherland*

James Joyce was born into a country dominated by England, and the cause of Irish freedom captured his imagination at an early age. The spokesman for this cause was Charles Stewart Parnell, who became a heroic figure in Joyce's imagination. It is difficult for us today to recapture the intensity of the conflicting emotions which divided Irish life at the close of the nineteenth century. Probably the best evocation of these emotions is the famous Christmas dinner scene in *A Portrait of the Artist* (272-83), where the forces of nationalism and Catholicism clash before the eyes of the terrified Stephen.[7] At the center of this political and religious turmoil stood the figure of Parnell. Years after Parnell's death, when the audience at the Abbey Theatre was unruly, W. B. Yeats silenced them by intoning three words: "Charles . . . Stewart . . . Parnell." [8] The early years of Joyce's life were the years of Parnell's greatest influence and tragic fall. By 1889 the attempt to implicate Parnell in the Phoenix Park murders of 1882 had failed, and he was regarded as a national hero; but in the same year he was accused of adultery in the divorce suit of Captain O'Shea. At first it appeared that Parnell might weather this scandal, but a coalition of political enemies and devout Catholics ousted him from leadership of the Irish Parliamentary Party, and the rural population of Ireland turned against their hero with savage hatred. Even Parnell's lieutenant Tim Healy, who had vowed never to abandon his leader, finally turned against him. After a year of campaigning against his enemies, Parnell died on October 6, 1891.

When Parnell's body was brought to Dublin for burial, thousands of his devoted followers were waiting for a glimpse of the coffin. "It was taken from a deal case—'which was thrown aside,' writes St. John Ervine, 'but, as it fell, crowds seized it and tore it into fragments that they might have even that as a relic of him'— and carried to City Hall. It lay there under O'Connell's statue through a wet and stormy morning and noon, while thirty thousand people filed past and plucked an ivy-leaf from it." Later, at the cemetery, a meteor flashed across the sky as the coffin reached the bottom of the grave: "Many spectators saw, or as time passed believed they had seen, the portents." [9] Already Parnell was being converted in the Irish imagination into a type of the betrayed hero, the savior destroyed by his own people. Nearly a half-century later Yeats was to give this view its finest expression in his great poem, "Parnell's Funeral":

> But popular rage,
> *Hysterica passio* dragged this quarry down.
> None shared our guilt; nor did we play a part
> Upon a painted stage when we devoured his heart.
>
> Come, fix upon me that accusing eye.
> I thirst for accusation. All that was sung,
> All that was said in Ireland is a lie
> Bred out of the contagion of the throng,
> Saving the rhyme rats hear before they die.
> Leave nothing but the nothings that belong
> To this bare soul, let all men judge that can
> Whether it be an animal or a man.[10]

Joyce's father reacted bitterly to the "betrayal" of Parnell, and nine-year-old James was so affected that he wrote a poem attacking Healy called "Et Tu, Healy." His delighted father had the poem printed and distributed copies to his friends. None of these has survived, but we know from Joyce's brother Stanislaus that at the end of the poem "the dead Chief is likened to an eagle, looking down on the grovelling mass of Irish politicians from

> His quaint-perched aerie on the crags of Time
> Where the rude din of this . . . century
> Can trouble him no more.[11]

The young Joyce's sympathetic identification with Parnell had a profound effect on his developing personality. The arrogance and pride of the great hero, the fear of betrayal, and the hypocrisy of the "rabblement" were to become leading themes in Joyce's life. The fall of Parnell was Joyce's first intimation that Ireland could be "the old sow that eats her farrow." [12] As Joyce matured, the pattern of Parnell's life seemed a foreshadowing of his own career. In the bitter broadside "Gas from a Burner" (1912), which was occasioned by his frustrations in finding a publisher for *Dubliners,* Joyce linked his own fate with Parnell's:

[21]

But I owe a duty to Ireland:
I hold her honour in my hand,
This lovely land that always sent
Her writers and artists to banishment
And in a spirit of Irish fun
Betrayed her own leaders, one by one.
'Twas Irish humour, wet and dry,
Flung quicklime into Parnell's eye . . . (660)

And in the same year as "Gas from a Burner" Joyce wrote an article for a Trieste newspaper called "The Shade of Parnell," which ends with this bitter passage: "In his final desperate appeal to his countrymen, he begged them not to throw him as a sop to the English wolves howling around them. It redounds to their honour that they did not fail this appeal. They did not throw him to the English wolves; they tore him to pieces themselves."[13] We must conclude that the shade of Parnell haunted Joyce all his life; the legend of the betrayed hero was incorporated into that personal myth which the young Joyce developed as a defense against the demands of home, fatherland, and church.

"Et Tu, Healy" was the beginning of Joyce's cold contempt for the shabby realities of Irish nationalism, a contempt matched only by his dedication to its highest ideals. In the decade after Parnell's death, Joyce developed a protective arrogance and aloofness which were dramatically displayed in his refusal to join the general protest against Yeats's *Countess Cathleen*. In 1899, when Joyce was in his first year at University College, the movement for an Irish theater was launched with the production of *The Countess Cathleen*. The first performance of the play was interrupted by booing from a group of young students who claimed that it was blasphemous and unpatriotic (the Countess, representing Ireland, sells her soul to the devil in order to save her starving people). The next day the Catholic nationalists at University College prepared a letter of protest; Joyce's signature was requested, but he refused: he was repelled by the narrow-minded theological and patriotic zeal which prompted such a manifesto. He had witnessed, within his short lifetime, the destruction of Ireland's potential savior by an alliance of priests and politicians, and he had no sympathy for those who wished to sentimentalize Irish culture. The "New Ireland" movement was not for him. Instead, he wished to make Ireland a part of Europe and to introduce cosmopolitan standards of excellence. Joyce had not lost his deep attachment to his native land (the works of his next forty years testify to this attachment), but he had turned away from all provincial forms of patriotism, seeing them as destructive to the integrity of Ireland and to his personal integrity.

During his four years at University College Joyce cultivated a public personality, a *persona*, which was later systematized and subjected to critical irony in the last chapter of *A Portrait of the Artist*. As his alienation from home, fatherland, and church increased, Joyce found he needed such a public personality to compensate for the shabbiness of his private life and to protect himself from the powerful demands of Irish nationalism. An essential part of this defense against provincial morals and taste was Joyce's "continental" orientation: he expressed contempt for most contemporary Irish writers and took for his model the great Norwegian dramatist, Henrik Ibsen.

In April of 1900 Joyce, who was scarcely eighteen years old, scored a triumph over his classmates by publishing a review of Ibsen's latest play, *When We Dead Awaken,* in the influential *Fortnightly Review*.[14] The review was competently constructed; Joyce devoted much of his space to quotation and paraphrase, but his critical observations revealed a deep understanding of Ibsen's themes and methods. However, it is in the opening paragraph that we recognize Ibsen's personal appeal to the young Joyce: "Ibsen's power over two generations has been enhanced by his own reticence. Seldom, if at all, has he condescended to join battle with his enemies. It would appear as if the storm of fierce debate rarely broke in upon his wonderful calm. The conflicting voices have not influenced his work in the very smallest degree." [15] Ibsen's personal detachment and cosmopolitan vision were the goals behind Joyce's posturings and protests. At a time when most young Irish writers were imitating the softer tones of Yeats and drawing their materials from native sources, Joyce was looking to the Continent for inspiration. The *Fortnightly Review* article marked a turning point in Joyce's development; his work had been accepted (and paid for) by a distinguished London periodical, but—more importantly—it had elicited recognition from Ibsen himself. In a brief note to his English translator, William Archer, Ibsen said: "I have read or rather spelt out, a review by Mr. James Joyce in the *Fortnightly Review* which is very benevolent and for which I should greatly like to thank the author if only I had sufficient knowledge of the language." [16]

Elated by Ibsen's response, Joyce continued his study of Dano-Norwegian, and by March, 1901, he had sufficiently mastered the language to write a long letter to Ibsen—a letter which differs markedly in tone from the *Fortnightly Review* and lays bare the deeper motives in Joyce's admiration for Ibsen:

I have sounded your name defiantly through a college where it was either unknown or known faintly and darkly. I have claimed for you your rightful place in the history of the drama. I have shown what, as it seemed to me, was your highest excellence—your lofty impersonal power. . . . Do not think me a hero-worshipper. I am not so. And when I spoke of you, in debating-societies, and so forth, I enforced attention by no futile ranting.

But we always keep the dearest things to ourselves. I did not tell *them* what bound me closest to you. I did not say how what I could discern dimly of your life was my pride to see, how your battles inspired me—not the obvious material battles but those that were fought and won behind your forehead—how your wilful resolution to wrest the secret from life gave me heart, and how in your absolute indifference to public canons of art, friends and shibboleths you walked in the light of your inward heroism.[17]

From this letter we can understand how Ibsen joined Parnell in Joyce's imagination. Joyce felt that both men had led lives of allegory, and the figurative meaning of their lives became the foundation of his youthful *persona*. By emulating their "lofty impersonal power" and their "indifference to public canons of art, friends and shibboleths," Joyce hoped to attain their "inward heroism."

The insistence upon the true artist's indifference to the demands of country and religion which dominates Joyce's letter to Ibsen was intensified as his career at University College progressed. In October, 1901, it burst into the open when Joyce wrote an arrogant attack on the program of the Irish Literary Theatre. He had been pleased by its first offerings, especially *The Countess Cathleen,* but the Theatre had recently become blatantly nationalistic, and Joyce was infuriated when he learned that the future offerings would be completely Irish. He had hoped that Continental drama and standards would be introduced, and in his disillusionment he wrote a scornful essay attacking the Theatre's provincialism. He submitted the essay to *St. Stephen's*, a college magazine; but the editor and faculty adviser refused to publish it. It was printed at Joyce's expense under the title "The Day of the Rabblement." [18]

"The Day of the Rabblement" announces gloomily that the "vulgar devil" has "prevailed once more and the Irish Literary Theatre must now be considered the property of the rabblement of the most belated race in Europe." Ireland, a "nation which never advanced so far as a miracle-play," provides the artist with no literary model; he must, therefore, "look abroad" for inspiration. But the Irish dramatists have failed to look abroad. Even Yeats, the most talented of Ireland's writers, has been led by his "treacherous instinct of adaptability" to endorse a popular platform. Joyce's essay closes on a note of arrogant self-confidence:

. . . the Irish Literary Theatre by its surrender to the trolls has cut itself adrift from the line of advancement. Until he has freed himself from the mean influences about him—sodden enthusiasm and clever insinuation and every flattering influence of vanity and low ambition—no man is an artist at all. But his true servitude is that he inherits a will broken by doubt and a soul that yields up all its hate to a caress; and the most seeming-independent are those who are the first to reassume their bonds. But Truth deals largely with us. Elsewhere there are men who are worthy to carry on the tradition of the old master who is dying in Christiania. He has already found his successor in the writer of *Michael Kramer,* and the third minister will not be wanting when his hour comes. Even now that hour may be standing by the door.[19]

The old master was, of course, Ibsen; his successor was the German dramatist Gerhart Hauptmann, whom Joyce had translated; the third minister was James Joyce.

"The Day of the Rabblement" was a public gesture, an expression of Joyce's *persona;* but it was also a confession of personal disappointment. Joyce had hoped that his ambitions as a playwright and translator would coincide with those of the new Theatre, but it seemed that this cause—like every other—was destined to be betrayed by the Irish public. Before "The Day of the Rabblement" Joyce had thought of himself as a rebel within the framework of Irish society, as a native spokesman for Continental standards. But from this point on his thoughts began to dwell on the possibilities of escape as well as of defiance.

In the spring of his last year at University College (1902) Joyce delivered a paper on the nineteenth-century Irish poet James Clarence Mangan which goes beyond Byronic defiance to reveal the deeper motives for Joyce's rejection of Irish nationalism. Couched in an exotic, Pateresque style, and devoted to a neglected native artist, the essay is essentially a lyric argument for "silence, exile, and cunning." At the center of the essay stands the figure of Mangan, the victim of cheap moralism and narrowly conceived patriotism:

. . . when Mangan is remembered in his country (for he is sometimes spoken of in literary societies), his countrymen lament that such poetic faculty was mated with so little rectitude of conduct, surprised to find this faculty in a man whose vices were exotic and who was little of a patriot. Those who have written of him, have been scrupulous in holding the balance between the drunkard and the opium-eater, and have sought to discover whether learning or imposture lies behind such phrases as 'from the Ottoman' or 'from the Coptic': and save for this small remembrance, Mangan has been a stranger in his country, a rare and unsympathetic figure in the streets, where he is seen going forward alone like one who does penance for some ancient sin.[20]

But Joyce does not focus the entire essay on this provincialism of the Irish public, as he might have done in earlier years. Instead, he frames the essay with a summary of his developing esthetic, concentrating upon the distinction between Romanticism and Classicism later elaborated in *Stephen Hero;* and he subjects Mangan himself to searching criticism:

. . . Mangan is the type of his race. History encloses him so straitly that even his fiery moments do not set him free from it. He, too, cries out, in his life and in his mournful verses, against the injustice of despoilers, but never laments a deeper loss than the loss of plaids and ornaments. He inherits the latest and worst part of a legend upon which the line has never been drawn out and which divides against itself as it moves down the cycles. And because this tradition is so much with him he has accepted it with all its griefs and failures, and has not known how to change it, as the strong spirit knows, and so would bequeath it: the poet who hurls his anger against tyrants would establish upon the future an intimate and far more cruel tyranny. . . . An eager spirit would cast down with violence the high traditions of Mangan's race—love of sorrow for the sake of sorrow and despair and fearful menaces—but where their voice is a supreme entreaty to be borne with forbearance seems only a little grace; and what is so courteous and so patient as a great faith? [21]

The burden of this obscure passage, and of the whole essay, is that the artist who protests from within the confines of Irish life can only express himself in "fiery moments," in "great cries and gestures"; his protests will themselves be a Romantic form of "narrow and hysterical nationality." If the Irish artist is to achieve the Classical temper, which is "not the manner of any fixed age or of any fixed country" but a "constant state of the artistic mind," [22] he must place himself beyond the immediate demands of Irish life. In the involved argument of this essay we can trace the motions of Joyce's mind as he moves, half-consciously, toward acceptance of a life in exile. Although his departure from Dublin in December, 1902, was not intended to be permanent, Joyce did conceive of it as a flight from the circumstances which limited Mangan's achievement. The Mangan essay helps us to understand Joyce's conviction that "the shortest route to Tara is via Holyhead." [23] But for a fuller understanding of Joyce's complex relationship with his native land we must investigate his early experiences with Irish Catholicism.

III *Church*

Joyce once told his friend Frank Budgen: "You allude to me as a Catholic. Now for the sake of precision and to get the correct contour on me, you ought to allude to me as a Jesuit." [24] This qualification is an important one, for Joyce received all of his formal education from the Jesuits. He entered Clongowes Wood College while he was still considered an infant under canon law, and he remained under the sponsorship of the Jesuits for fourteen years, although their effective influence upon him ceased before he matriculated at University College in 1898. [25] At Clongowes Wood Joyce was younger than the other boys in his class, and he seems to have led the usual life of a boy sent to boarding school at too early an age. Most of the Fathers were kind to him, and although the "pandybat" incident described in *A Portrait of the Artist* (293-304) actually occurred, it does not seem to have been typical of Joyce's life at the school. After his initial homesickness wore off, Joyce settled into the routine of the school and began to distinguish himself in class. During his three years at Clongowes Wood he received an excellent education and absorbed—apparently without question—the basic beliefs of Catholicism.

The most important religious experiences of Joyce's life occurred at Belvedere College, which he attended from the age of eleven to the age of sixteen. Belvedere was less fashionable than Clongowes Wood; already the decline of the family fortune was making itself felt in James's life. At Belvedere Joyce was an outstanding scholar, and it was not long before the authorities had singled him out as a possible candidate for the priesthood. During his last two years at the college Joyce was elected Prefect of the Sodality; that is to say, he was elected head of a group of students who banded together for the purposes of devotion and mutual help. This election is strong evidence of the seriousness with which he considered a vocation in the priesthood. As Prefect of the Sodality it was his duty—in the words of the Jesuit manual— to "excel the other members of the Sodality in virtue" and to "observe with the greatest diligence not only the rules of his own office but also the common rules, those especially that relate to the frequentation of the sacraments, confessing his sins, and receiving the Blessed Eucharist more frequently than the others; and he should take care to advance the Sodality in the way of virtue and Christian perfection, more by example even than by words." [26]

Joyce's duties as Prefect of the Sodality were analogous in their own way to the functions of the priest, and it is from these days that we must date his view of the artist as a secular priest, an attitude that had a profound impact on his artistic development. Of course, Joyce was not an ideal Prefect. Like many adolescents, he was torn between the spiritual demands of the Sodality and a growing interest in physical love; and at some time close to his election as Prefect he had his first sexual experience. This episode was followed by the retreat and mortification later described in A Portrait of the Artist.[27] However, it would be a great mistake to read the corresponding sections of A Portrait as faithful autobiography. While at Belvedere Joyce went on at least five religious retreats—in contrast to a single retreat in the Portrait—and of these only the retreat of December, 1896, seems to have produced anything like the harrowing effects described in the novel. Furthermore, there is no evidence that Joyce committed frequent sins of the flesh at this time. We are forced to conclude that the charting of Stephen's religious life in A Portrait of *the Artist* is the least autobiographical part of the novel. Joyce took great liberties with the facts of his own youth in order to construct a neat pattern of acceptance and rejection. For example, in the *Portrait* Stephen's rejection of the priesthood as a possible vocation is treated as if it were simultaneous with his rejection of Catholicism; in Joyce's life the two decisions were separated by a considerable period of time. While still at Belvedere Joyce decided that he could not be a priest, but the loss of his faith was a more gradual process. There seems to have been an intermediate period when Joyce was still bound to the Church by esthetic ties —a love of mystery and of ritual—while at the same time he was gradually awakening to the possibility of being an artist, a priest of life. Stephen Dedalus' vision of the wading girl in *A Portrait of the Artist* (432) was based on an ecstatic experience Joyce had during his last year at Belvedere, when even the esthetic appeal of the Church was waning;[28] by the time he reached University College his conscious allegiance to the Jesuits had ended.

I say "conscious allegiance," because Joyce's emotional involvement with the Church never ended. The Jesuits had wrought better than they knew. The main principle of Jesuit education is conformity of the individual teachers to a traditional system of instruction, and in the Jesuit schools which Joyce attended he learned fixed methods for handling every intellectual problem, methods buttressed by theory and proved by generations of teachers. In 1892 the Jesuit General defined Jesuit education as "training of the mind," and he emphasized that the essence of this training lay not in the "subject matter" but in "the 'form,' or spirit of the system." [29] Jesuit institutions such as Belvedere College aimed at giving their students a form or pattern for dissecting and resolving intellectual problems, and we can see evidence of this analytic process in Joyce's methods of composition.[30] The education Joyce received from the Jesuits was excellent preparation for the priesthood, but it was also fine training for the artist.

Although Joyce consciously rejected Catholicism before the age of twenty-one and held fast to this decision all his life, I do not think it is a paradox to call him a "Catholic" writer. His mind remained—as Cranly says of Stephen's mind in the *Portrait* (510) —supersaturated with the religion in which he refused to believe. As Yeats once remarked, "Joyce never lost his Catholic sense of sin";[31] neither did he lose the habits of thought and language learned at Clongowes Wood, Belvedere, and University College. Throughout his works Catholicism is a pervasive force, manifesting itself through metaphor and symbol. When a lady once asked Joyce if he had found a satisfactory substitute for Catholicism, Joyce replied: "Madam, I have lost my faith, I have not lost my mind." [32] The Catholic world-view provides the rational framework for all of Joyce's art.

Although Joyce perverted and transformed the rites of the Church, they remained for him the most effective expression of life's mysteries; and his mature conception of the artist's role was conditioned by his early admiration for the priesthood. Joyce saw the artist as a surrogate priest, whose office depends upon his ability to understand and reveal spiritual realities. As we shall see in the next chapter, the heart of Joyce's esthetic theory is his notion of the "epiphany," the moment when spiritual reality is manifested in artistic form, just as the incarnate Word was revealed to the Wise Men. For Joyce the artistic process was "eucharistic," a transformation of spirit into matter; when, on his fiftieth birthday, he was presented with a cake topped by a candy replica of *Ulysses,* Joyce paused before cutting it and said: "*Hoc est enim corpus meum* [This is my body]." [33] The metaphor is both blasphemous and exact. Although Joyce modeled his youthful *persona* after the examples of Parnell and Ibsen, the strength to maintain it—and ultimately to surmount it—came from a different source. Stanislaus Joyce, whose rejection of the Church was much more violent than his brother's, has said the last word on this subject: "I confess I have no better explanation to offer of [my brother's] triumphant struggle to preserve his rectitude as an artist in the midst of illness and disappointment, in abject poverty and disillusionment, than this, that he who has loved God intensely in his youth will never love anything less. The definition may change, the service abides." [34]

CHAPTER 2

Early Works

I *Poetry*

JAMES JOYCE was first and last a poet. His earliest literary
effort, at the age of nine, was a poem in honor of the dead
Parnell; his final achievement was the great poetic tribute to Anna
Livia Plurabelle which closes *Finnegans Wake.* Poetry was the
natural medium for the expression of Joyce's deepest emotions.
After the completion of *Chamber Music* in 1904-5 he wrote only a
few short lyrics—the thirteen poems collected as *Pomes Penyeach*
(1927), and *"Ecce Puer"* (1932)—but each of these is a revelation
of his inner life. "She Weeps Over Rahoon," for example, was
written after Joyce and his wife Nora had paid a visit (during
their 1912 trip to Ireland) to the grave of Nora's early sweetheart,
Michael Bodkin, who was the model for Michael Furey in "The
Dead." [1] The poem expresses Joyce's vision of the relationship between the living husband and the dead lover in Nora's mind.
"Bahnhofstrasse," written in 1918, links Joyce's sense of lost youth
with his failing sight (Joyce had his first attack of glaucoma on
the Bahnhofstrasse, a Zurich street). [2] The other lyrics in *Pomes
Penyeach* are equally personal in their origins.

Most moving of all the mature poems is *"Ecce Puer,"* which was
written out of Joyce's despair over the recent death of his father
and joy at the birth of his grandson. [3] In it the biblical overtones
enlarge the poem into a commentary on the whole course of
Joyce's life:

> Of the dark past
> A child is born;
> With joy and grief
> My heart is torn.
>
> Calm in his cradle
> The living lies.

May love and mercy
Unclose his eyes!

Young life is breathed
On the glass;
The world that was not
Comes to pass.

A child is sleeping:
An old man gone.
O, father forsaken,
Forgive your son!   (663)

When confronted with *"Ecce Puer"* and with the more successful lyrics in *Pomes Penyeach,* we may wonder why Joyce directed
his poetic impulse into the creation of fiction; the answer lies in
the nature of his early poetry and its relationship to the more mature works, especially *Dubliners.*

In the mid-1890's Joyce collected some of his schoolboy poems
under the title *Moods;* none of these verses has survived, but they
must have been similar to the poems written around 1900 under
the title *Shine and Dark.*[4] The few verses from *Shine and Dark*
which were not lost or destroyed are highly imitative, derived
from the vague Romanticism of the 1890's. According to Joyce's
brother Stanislaus, the villanelle which Stephen Dedalus com-
poses in *A Portrait of the Artist* (483-91) was one of these early
poems;[5] and we can learn a great deal about Joyce's mature attitude toward *Shine and Dark* from his ironic treatment of the
villanelle in *A Portrait.* In contrast to Stephen's sophisticated esthetic, the poem is diffuse and unoriginal. The pretentious description of the creative process is deflated by the villanelle itself,
the first line of which echoes Ben Jonson. When Stephen takes his
morning walk across the city and passes "a grimy marine dealer's
shop across the Liffey" he repeats "the song by Ben Jonson which
begins: *I was not wearier where I lay*" (436). If we compare the
full song from Jonson's *Vision of Delight* with the opening of Stephen's villanelle, Joyce's ironic intention becomes apparent:

I was not wearier where I lay
By frozen Tithon's side to-night,
Than I am willing now to stay,

[32]

> And be a part of your delight.
> But I am urgéd by the Day,
> Against my will, to bid you come away.
>
> . . . .
>
> Are you not weary of ardent ways,
> Lure of the fallen seraphim?
> Tell me no more of enchanted days.

By contrasting Jonson's controlled lines with Stephen's diffuse expression of *fin de siècle* weariness, Joyce has exposed his hero's pretensions and, incidentally, provided us with some acute criticism of *Shine and Dark*.

Most of the poems in *Chamber Music* were written between 1902 and 1904, although the volume was not published until 1907. Yeats viewed these poems as the work of "a young man who is practicing his instrument, taking pleasure in the mere handling of the stops," [6] and this is certainly the dominant impression conveyed by *Chamber Music*. There are obvious debts to the Romantic poets (XXVI), and some passages suggest the "mood" poetry of the 1890's (especially II, which dates from the *Shine and Dark* period [7]). Some of the verses are fine imitations of the Elizabethan lyric (VI); others are modeled on the Irish folk song (XXXI). Joyce was an excellent singer who loved Elizabethan music, and it was his hope—later fulfilled—that the poems of *Chamber Music* would be set to music by "someone who knows old English music such as I like." [8] He thought of *Chamber Music* as a "suite" of songs, and the collection is filled with musical imagery; more importantly, the songs are held in place by a musical structure of leitmotivs and recurrent themes. There is a pervasive debt to Verlaine, whose "Art Poétique"—with its emphasis on musical form and the nuance—stands behind the whole collection.

But it would be a mistake to think of *Chamber Music* solely in terms of imitated styles. There are occasions when Joyce, like the best of the Elizabethan sonneteers, uses the conventional styles for new effects. Such an occasion is Poem XII. According to Stanislaus Joyce, this lyric grew out of an experience his brother had one evening in 1904. A young girl whom James admired remarked that the pale, mist-encircled moon looked "tearful." James replied that "It looks to me like the chubby hooded face of some jolly fat

Capuchin." After the girl had left, Joyce "tore open a cigarette-box and standing under a street lamp wrote the two verses of the song on the inside of the box." [9]

What counsel has the hooded moon
   Put in thy heart, my shyly sweet,
Of Love in ancient plenilune,
   Glory and stars beneath his feet—
A sage that is but kith and kin
With the comedian Capuchin?

Believe me rather that am wise
   In disregard of the divine,
A glory kindles in those eyes
   Trembles to starlight. Mine, O Mine!
No more be tears in moon or mist
For thee, sweet sentimentalist.   (635)

Here the argument against sentimentality has been expressed through a deliberate clash of styles. The girl sees the mist-encircled moon as a conventional emblem of Love's sad mysteries, and her view is cast in appropriate language. But Joyce, in the manner of Jules Laforgue, converts the "hooded moon" of convention into the startling image of a "comedian Capuchin," thus deflating the sentimentality of "Love in ancient plenilune" and reinforcing his theme of earthly glory. This deliberate interplay of styles is not a frequent method in *Chamber Music*—Joyce is most often a prisoner of the style he imitates—but it deserves attention as a sign of his growing command of language, and of his deep-felt need for irony.

In *Stephen Hero* the young poet says that "in his expressions of love he found himself compelled to use what he called the feudal terminology and as he could not use it with the same faith and purpose as animated the feudal poets themselves he was compelled to express his love a little ironically." [10] This is an accurate summation of Joyce's dilemma in *Chamber Music:* he finds himself trapped between commitment to the inherited style and distrust of the emotions it expresses. The method of Poem XII provided one escape from this dilemma.

Another atypical poem which demands attention is XXXVI, "I hear an army." In this lyric there is no irony; Joyce has fused the inherited styles into a sure form of his own. The emphasis is entirely on sound, not sight—"hear," "thunder," "cry," "moan," "clanging," "shouting"—yet the total impact of the poem is that of a powerful visual image. As the poem develops, the scene struggles into sight like the army out of the sea; the materials of nightmare have been given precise expression. It is not surprising that when Ezra Pound compiled his *Des Imagistes* anthology in 1913 he included "I hear an army" and praised it for its "objective" form.[11] Long before the Imagist "movement" came into being, Joyce had broken his own bondage to the 1890's and had achieved a style which would satisfy the Imagist ideal of objectivity and concentration. In his poetry, as in his fiction, Joyce anticipated the direction of twentieth-century literature. Poems such as "I hear an army" prepared Joyce for *Dubliners,* just as the Imagist movement in modern poetry helped prepare the reading public for Joyce's stories.[12]

And yet, in spite of his successes in *Chamber Music,* Joyce reacted violently against the work. By 1906 he was referring to it contemptuously as a "young man's book," and wishing that he could find another title which would "to a certain extent repudiate the book, without altogether disparaging it."[13] And in 1907 he nearly canceled publication, explaining: "All that kind of thing is false."[14] How can we account for this change in attitude? One answer, probably the most important one, is that Joyce was by nature a sentimentalist, and that this sentimentalism was exposed in the revelations of lyric poetry. *Chamber Music* always loomed large in Joyce's sentimental life, especially in his relationship with Nora (after a reconciliation with Nora in 1909 Joyce sent her a parchment copy of *Chamber Music,* with her initials and his entwined on the cover, accompanied by a sentimental letter).[15] But in his art Joyce was determined to control his sentimentality, and to accomplish this aim he needed the greater objectivity—the ironic contexts—provided by fiction. The deflation of Stephen's villanelle in *A Portrait of the Artist* is a fine example of the control Joyce sought.

As Joyce matured, he channeled his lyric talent into the forms of fiction, and we must see this development as part of the process which translated the self-revelations of *Stephen Hero* into the more impersonal form of *Portrait.* When Joyce told his brother in 1906 that "a page of *A Little Cloud* gives me more pleasure than all my verses," [16] he was obviously thinking of the stricter control provided by the new work. That balance of sympathy and irony which he had attained fitfully in *Chamber Music* is present throughout *Dubliners*.

Another aspect of *Chamber Music* which indicates the direction of Joyce's development is the collection's general design. As the songs accumulated, Joyce made several tentative arrangements of them, the last and most important of these being an arrangement of the first thirty-four songs which dates from 1905. However, by late 1906 he was so indifferent to the fate of the collection that he allowed his brother Stanislaus to determine the published sequence. Stanislaus gave the thirty-six songs a musical arrangement, hoping "to suggest a closed episode of youth and love," and Joyce accepted this without comment; [17] however, the earlier arrangement of thirty-four songs was obviously still in mind when he wrote in 1909 to an Irish composer who was setting some of the lyrics to music. "The central song is XIV after which the movement is all downwards until XXXIV which is vitally the end of the book. XXXV and XXXVI are tailpieces just as I and III are preludes." [18]

The fact that the songs of *Chamber Music* are amenable to several "narrative" arrangements should caution us against too strict an interpretation of the collection's general design, but we can discern various patterns in the "movement" of the songs. They trace the evolution of an imaginary love affair, from initial harmony to final separation, and they also chart—on an allegorical level—the journey of the soul from security to isolation. These patterns are reinforced by allusions to the cycle of the seasons from spring to winter, and to the day's progress from dawn to dusk.[19] Furthermore, repeated motifs (such as that of "earth and air") bind the individual songs together. I do not wish to place too much stress on these structural rhythms, but only to point out that they are related to the much stricter patterns which give an architectural order to *Dubliners*. Like the fitful resorts to irony, they remind us of Joyce's desire to control the lyric impulse.

II   *The Epiphanies*

Joyce's epiphanies form a bridge between the early poetry and the early fiction, and help us to understand the formative stages of his art.[20] Throughout his artistic career, Joyce recorded crucial fragments of dialogue or personal experience, carefully hoarded them, and finally—when he had determined their "spiritual" significance—used them as organizing centers for his art. However, in this chapter I shall be concerned only with those epiphanies written between 1900 and 1904, when Joyce thought of them as separate works.

When he first began to collect his epiphanies Joyce regarded them, in the words of his brother Stanislaus, as "little errors and gestures—mere straws in the wind—by which people betrayed the very things they were most careful to conceal." [21] The earliest epiphanies were brief sketches, objective in form and deliberately fragmentary; but as Joyce's interest in the subconscious increased, and as his "theory" of the epiphany became more elaborate, these dramatic sketches were joined by lyrical passages expressing a mood and by accounts of dreams.[22] Joyce came to think of the epiphanies as moments of artistic radiance, and he advanced this definition in *Stephen Hero*: "By an epiphany he [Stephen Daedalus] meant a sudden spiritual manifestation, whether in the vulgarity of speech or of gesture or in a memorable phase of the mind itself. He believed that it was for the man of letters to record these epiphanies with extreme care, seeing that they themselves are the most delicate and evanescent of moments." [23] In this passage Stephen seems to be distinguishing between the dramatic epiphanies ("the vulgarity of speech or of gesture") and the lyrical epiphanies which record "a memorable phase of the mind itself."

The best way to understand Joyce's notion of the epiphany is to see how specific epiphanies were incorporated into his fiction. The following epiphany, one of the most dramatic, was reworked to make a famous and magnificently effective part of the opening to *A Portrait of the Artist:*

[BRAY: in the parlour of the house in Martello Terrace]
MR VANCE—(*comes in with a stick*) . . . O, you know, he'll have to apologise, Mrs. Joyce.
MRS JOYCE—O yes . . . Do you hear that, Jim?
MR VANCE—Or else—if he doesn't—the eagles'll come and pull out his eyes.
MRS JOYCE—O, but I'm sure he will apologise.
JOYCE—(*under the table, to himself*)

—Pull out his eyes.
    Apologise,
    Apologise,
Pull out his eyes.

    Apologise,
Pull out his eyes,
Pull out his eyes,
    Apologise.[24]

Even as an isolated incident this epiphany is an arresting expression of a sensitive child's confrontation with authority; but the fragment does not become a "revelation," a radiant image, until it reaches its place in *Portrait* (246) as an introduction to the great themes of guilt and submission. By itself the fragment could only have been "radiant" to Joyce, since its context is his life. The epiphanies are like an artist's *trouvailles;* their significance lies in the writer's recognition of their potentialities, but these potentialities must be communicated in some fashion. This personal quality of the isolated epiphany is even clearer in lyric passages such as the following, which was incorporated almost without change into the diary at the end of *Portrait:*

The spell of arms and voices—the white arms of roads, their promise of close embraces, and the black arms of tall ships that stand against the moon, their tale of distant nations. They are held out to say: We are alone,—come. And the voices say with them, We are your people. And the air is thick with their company as they call to me their kinsman, making ready to go, shaking the wings of their exultant and terrible youth.[25]

When read as an isolated passage this epiphany is simply a haunting but somewhat overwritten "prose poem," but in the context of *Portrait* (where it is qualified by Joyce's irony) it becomes a true "manifestation" of Stephen's romantic ambitions. My point is that, as separate works, the epiphanies were "spiritual manifestations" only to Joyce, but that they were transformed into radiant moments when he processed them into his mature art.

In contrast to the concentrated but enigmatic epiphanies, Joyce's long prose work of this early period—*Stephen Hero*—is prolix and blatantly explicit. This work can be most fruitfully criticized in relation to its successor, *A Portrait of the Artist,* and I shall return to it in Chapter Four. But it may be illuminating, in connection with our discussion of the epiphanies, to pause and take a preliminary measure of *Stephen Hero*. The novel's style and methods are evident in the following passage, which ends with one of the epiphanies: [26]

The inexpressibly mean way in which his sister had been buried inclined Stephen to consider rather seriously the claims of water and fire to be the last homes of dead bodies. The entire apparatus of the State seemed to him at fault from its first to its last operation. No young man can contemplate the fact of death with extreme satisfaction and no young man, specialised by fate or her stepsister chance for an organ of sensitiveness and intellectiveness, can contemplate the network of falsities and trivialities which make up the funeral of a dead burgher without extreme disgust. For some days after the funeral Stephen, clothed in second-hand clothes of two shades of black, had to receive sympathies. Many of these sympathies proceeded from casual friends of the family. Nearly all the men said 'And how is the poor mother bearing it?' and nearly all the women said 'It's a great trial for your mother': and the sympathies were always uttered in the same listless unconvincing monotone. McCann was also sympathetic. He came over to Stephen while that young man was looking into a haberdasher's window at some ties and wondering why the Chinese chose yellow as a colour of mourning. He shook hands briskly with Stephen:
—I was sorry to hear of the death of your sister . . . sorry we didn't know in time . . . to have been at the funeral.
Stephen released his hand gradually and said:
—O, she was very young . . . a girl.
McCann released his hand at the same rate of release, and said:
—Still . . . it hurts.
The acme of unconvincingness seemed to Stephen to have been reached at that moment.[27]

This is obviously not very successful. The style is flat and un-rhythmical, and there is a good deal of youthful editorializing. The point of view is uncertain; we are supposed to follow Stephen's reactions, but Joyce's voice breaks through in the third sentence. Obviously Joyce is too close to his materials, which are the events of his own life. The death of his brother has been turned into that of Stephen's sister, and his friend Skeffington has become McCann; but these are merely mechanical changes. The epiphany, which must have been jotted down shortly after the death of

Joyce's brother George in March, 1902, is unaltered by the context. It is still an illustration, a personal observation, not a "showing forth" or a "sudden spiritual manifestation." Biography has not been transformed into anything resembling the young Joyce's artistic ideal.

The parts of *Stephen Hero* which have survived are important for what they tell us of Joyce's personality and his artistic development, but they can hardly claim our attention on any other level. It would seem that although the brief epiphanies and the sprawling *Stephen Hero* may, in their intentions, represent esthetic extremes (the sudden moment of revelation, the carefully developed novel of environment and motivation), they fail because Joyce had not yet learned how to give objective form to the relationships existing in his own mind. But even as *Stephen Hero* was being written Joyce was mastering, in the stories of *Dubliners,* the necessary techniques for producing an extended work of fiction organized around moments of intense symbolic significance. We may assume that he abandoned *Stephen Hero* in 1905-6 because it could not stand comparison with the short stories of *Dubliners.* But before we look at these stories we must examine the esthetic theories of the young James Joyce.

III *Criticism*

Joyce's critical theories have probably received more attention than any other aspect of his early work.[28] This interest is understandable; Stephen's esthetic speculations in *A Portrait of the Artist* are an essential part of the novel's structure and have provided some of the catchwords of modern criticism. But we must guard against two dangers in discussing Joyce's esthetic: first, the danger of identifying Stephen's beliefs with those of the mature Joyce; and second, the danger of using a youthful theory to explain the entire course of Joyce's development. Already in *Stephen Hero* Joyce is reworking his theories to meet the demands of characterization and structural symmetry—his early essays on "Drama and Life" and "James Clarence Mangan" are blended into one—but we can still assume that the basic tenets of Stephen's esthetic reflect Joyce's current beliefs. However, in the process of turning *Stephen Hero* into *Portrait* Joyce achieved the same perspective on his early esthetic that he achieved on other aspects of his youth, and we cannot say that the full esthetic presented in *Por-*

trait is that of Joyce at the age of thirty. Significantly, the notion of the epiphany—perhaps the most important of the early theories —was omitted from *Portrait,* probably because Joyce did not wish to subject it to the irony that surrounds Stephen's artistic ambitions.

Our best plan in this chapter will be to disregard the esthetic discussion in *Portrait* and concentrate upon Joyce's early essays and the Paris and Pola notebooks, borrowing judiciously from *Stephen Hero* wherever necessary.[29] In this way we shall be able to see the esthetic for what it was: a starting point. The temptation to interpret Joyce's full achievement in terms of the early esthetic is a strong one, but it must be resisted.

Much has been made of Joyce's debt to Aquinas, but I think it significant that this debt looms larger in the fiction than in the essays and notebooks. As we shall see later, some of the important tenets of Joyce's esthetic are modifications of Aristotelian theory, but the relationship to Aquinas strikes me as more tentative. Aquinas provided Joyce with some hints, with materials to be manipulated; but his greatest importance was as an "authority." Like Stephen, Joyce wished to claim that he had reconciled Classical and Christian theory. In fact, Joyce's chief debt to scholasticism may have been in the area of style and form of argument. In *A Portrait of the Artist* Stephen poses this problem:

—*If a man hacking in fury at a block of wood . . . make there an image of a cow, is that image a work of art? If not, why not?*
—That's a lovely one, said Lynch, laughing again. That has the true scholastic stink. (480-81)

This exchange grew out of a question-and-answer in the 1903 Paris notebook.

QUESTION: If a man hacking in fury at a block of wood make there an image of a cow (say) has he made a work of art?
ANSWER: The image of a cow made by a man hacking in fury at a block of wood is a human disposition of sensible matter but it is not a human disposition of sensible matter for an aesthetic end. Therefore it is not a work of art.[30]

However seriously Joyce may have taken this problem in 1903, in *A Portrait of the Artist* it is qualified by irony and serves to characterize Stephen's humorless scholasticism.

Joyce's early theories are best considered under three related headings: the role of the artist, the form of the work he produces, and the reaction of the audience to that work. The early Joyce did not believe, as does Stephen in *A Portrait,* that the artist, "like the God of the creation, remains within or beyond or above his handiwork, invisible, refined out of existence, indifferent, paring his fingernails" (481-82). In his essay on the Irish poet James Clarence Mangan (1902) Joyce speaks of Mangan's works as expressions of his personality:

Many of his essays are pretty fooling when read once, but one cannot but discern some fierce energy beneath the banter, which follows up the phrases with no good intent, and there is a likeness between the desperate writer, himself the victim of too dexterous torture, and the contorted writing. . . . the best of what he has written makes its appeal surely, because it was conceived by the imagination which he called, I think, the mother of things, whose dream are we, who imageth us to herself, and to ourselves, and imageth herself in us—the power before whose breath the mind in creation is (to use Shelley's image[31]) as a fading coal. Though even in the best of Mangan the presence of alien emotions is sometimes felt the presence of an imaginative personality reflecting the light of imaginative beauty is more vividly felt.[32]

The "imaginative personality" can only be preserved, however, through a studied disregard for popular demands: "the artist, though he may employ the crowd, is very careful to isolate himself."[33] "If an artist courts the favour of the multitude," Joyce says in "The Day of the Rabblement," thinking of the nationalistic demands of the Irish literary movement, "he cannot escape the contagion of its fetichism and deliberate self-deception, and if he joins in a popular movement he does so at his own risk."[34] Didacticism is the enemy of art: "a man who writes a book cannot be excused by his good intentions, or by his moral character; he enters into a region where there is question of the written word, and it is well that this should be borne in mind, now that the region of literature is assailed so fiercely by the enthusiast and the doctrinaire."[35]

But this isolation from the popular currents of the age, this rejection of didacticism, does not mean that the artist is indifferent —or that art is without moral value. Speaking of Ibsen's handling of a situation which might offend the moralists, Joyce says: "Ibsen treats it, as indeed he treats all things, with large insight, artistic restraint, and sympathy. He sees it steadily and whole, as from a great height, with perfect vision and an angelic dispassionateness, with the sight of one who may look on the sun with open eyes." [36]

This passage echoes, perhaps unconsciously, Matthew Arnold's plea for a disinterestedness such as that of Sophocles, "who saw life steadily, and saw it whole." [37] Disinterestedness does not imply indifference; rather, it is the ability to rise above local passions and to "see the object as in itself it really is." [38] Only by being dispassionate can the artist achieve that wholeness of expression which was Arnold's, and Joyce's, ideal. This objective attitude is a far cry from the sterile "indifference," the Flaubertian pose, of Stephen in the *Portrait*. The young Joyce may often have displayed Stephen's arrogance and aloofness in his actions, but these qualities were not part of his esthetic.

It seems clear that Joyce's esthetic aim was that of so many post-Romantic critics: he wished to restate the ideals of Classical art in terms of his own personality and the conditions of modern life. Unlike Arnold, whose Classicism was an attempt to regain the past, Joyce hoped to direct the natural tendencies of modern literature toward Classical ends. This aim is well stated in *Stephen Hero*, in the passage which follows some rather modish speculation on the artist as a mediator between the "world of experience" and the "world of dreams":

Such a theory might easily have led its deviser to the acceptance of spiritual anarchy in literature had he not at the same time insisted on the classical style. A classical style, he said, is the syllogism of art, the only legitimate process from one world to another. Classicism is not the manner of any fixed age or of any fixed country: it is a constant state of the artistic mind. It is a temper of security and satisfaction and patience. The romantic temper, so often and so grievously misinterpreted and not more by others than by its own, is an insecure, unsatisfied, impatient temper which sees no fit abode here for its ideals and chooses therefore to behold them under insensible figures. As a result of this choice it comes to disregard certain limitations. Its figures are blown to wild adventures, lacking the gravity of solid bodies, and the mind that has conceived them ends by disowning them. The classical temper on the other hand, ever mindful of limitations, chooses rather to bend upon these present things and so to work upon them and fashion them that the quick intelligence may go beyond them to their meaning which is still unuttered. In this method the sane and joyful spirit issues forth and achieves imperishable perfection, nature assisting with her goodwill and thanks.[39]

This "classical temper" can only be achieved by the disinterested artist whose "sane and joyful spirit" is reflected in the formal qualities of his art.

Turning now from the artist to his product, we find that Joyce abandoned the conventional definitions of genres which are derived from an examination of subject and structure; instead, he defined the major "conditions" of art in terms of the artist's relationship to his creation: ". . . There are three conditions of art: the lyrical, the epical and the dramatic. That art is lyrical whereby the artist sets forth the image in immediate relation to himself; that art is epical whereby the artist sets forth the image in mediate relation to himself and to others; that art is dramatic whereby the artist sets forth the image in immediate relation to others. . . ." [40]

These broad definitions, which apply in theory to every form of art, have received far too much attention. The lyrical-epical-dramatic pattern has been applied to Joyce's entire artistic career, and he has been both condemned for failing to make *Finnegans Wake* "dramatic" and praised for his skilful synthesis of the three modes in the *Wake*. Such pat applications strike me as absurd; the mature work of an artist should not be judged in the framework of his youthful esthetic. It is revealing that the Stephen of *Stephen Hero* is "not greatly perturbed because he could not decide for himself whether a portrait was a work of epical art or not," [41] whereas in *A Portrait of the Artist* Stephen treats the distinctions in a more elaborate fashion (480-81). The most interesting aspect of Joyce's theory is his recognition that the traditional definitions of kind and genre have broken down, and his attempt to re-establish them on the basis of the artist's psychology—the creator's "distancing" of his materials.

As for the qualities of the beautiful work, Joyce follows his tags from Aquinas—*integritas, consonantia, claritas*—and defines the beautiful in relation to the act of apprehension.[42] The movement is from cognition to recognition to satisfaction.[43] First we must understand the integrity of the object, its uniqueness. Then we analyze the object in relation to other objects and to itself, tracing the symmetry of its structure; this leads to a recognition of its harmonious unity. Finally, we reach the satisfaction provided by the object's *claritas:* its essential nature is revealed.

After the analysis which discovers the second quality the mind makes the only logically possible synthesis and discovers the third quality. This is the moment which I call epiphany. First we recognise that the object is *one* integral thing, then we recognise that it is an organised composite structure, a *thing* in fact: finally, when the relation of the parts is exquisite, when the parts are adjusted to the special point, we recognise that it is *that* thing which it is. Its soul, its whatness, leaps to us from the vestment of its appearance. The soul of the commonest object, the structure of which is so adjusted, seems to us radiant. The object achieves its epiphany.[44]

Thus the epiphany, which stands at the end of the process of apprehension, is the goal of the artist. But even in his early esthetic Joyce is aware that this timeless moment of revelation must be apprehended in time: the epiphany is dependent upon its context.

Joyce's comments on the work of art are basically *psychological*. The conditions or kinds of art are determined by the relationship between the artist and the image; beauty is defined through analysis of the act of apprehension. In the void between lies the work of art itself. Like so many esthetic theories, Joyce's is weakest at the point where it touches the practical problems of creation.

In what I have called the third section of his esthetic Joyce considers the nature of comedy and tragedy, dealing with them in psychological terms.[45] Bad tragedy incites loathing; it moves us to action. But the terror and pity excited by proper tragedy "hold us in rest, as it were, by fascination":

When tragic art makes my body to shrink terror is not my feeling because I am urged from rest, and moreover this art does not show me what is grave, I mean what is constant and irremediable in human fortunes nor does it unite me with any secret cause for it shows me only what is unusual and remediable and it unites me with a cause only too manifest. Nor is an art properly tragic which would move me to prevent human suffering any more than an art is properly tragic which would move me in anger against some manifest cause of human suffering.[46]

Similarly, bad comedy moves us to desire, but true comedy excites a "joy which holds us in rest." These observations bring Joyce to his fundamental statement: "All art . . . is static for the feelings of terror and pity on the one hand and of joy on the other hand are feelings which arrest us." [47]

"Stasis" is Joyce's modification of the Aristotelian *catharsis*, and it applies to both comedy and tragedy; but, unlike Aristotle, Joyce has nothing to say of the particular forms of comedy and tragedy. Instead, he is concerned with "comic" and "tragic" effects, which can be found in fiction as well as in drama; and the way is left open for the blending of comic and tragic effects in a single work. Joyce seems to believe that in their final psychological impact comedy and tragedy are the same, and that all esthetic experiences depend on the common quality of "stasis." "Stasis" is the end of the process which begins with the artist's disinterested role, and it is the essential prerequisite for the apprehension of beauty. This is not an amoral concept, but it does exclude the "kinetic" effects of didactic art. Behind Joyce's esthetic lies the conviction that the contemplation of a work of art does not lead to good; it is a "good" in itself. "Art for art's sake" has been reconciled with the Aristotelian *catharsis* to produce an esthetic position which remains—after all its limitations have been stated—the most impressive part of Joyce's early achievement.

CHAPTER 3

Dubliners

T HE stories in *Dubliners* were written between 1904 and 1907, when Joyce was between the ages of twenty-two and twenty-five. As early as February, 1906, a preliminary version of the collection (lacking "Two Gallants," "A Little Cloud," and "The Dead") was accepted for publication by the London firm of Grant Richards; but the printer objected to certain passages and refused to fulfill his contract. Joyce then launched into a battle to have his book printed as he had written it; but it was not until nine years later, after *Dubliners* had passed through the hands of three publishers, that the collection was finally published.

The difficulties Joyce encountered in bringing *Dubliners* to the public provide a fascinating record of late-Victorian prejudice and prudery, with the objections of the various printers and publishers falling into three classes: they were shocked by passages of mild profanity; they objected to the use of real names and places; and they balked at a few political and religious references. Joyce in his turn was often illogical or imprudent, especially when the dispute reinforced his growing sense of alienation and frustration. After a lapse of fifty years the details of Joyce's publishing difficulties are interesting only in so far as they illuminate his personality and the nature of his art, and it is in this light that we must view his stubborn refusal to alter particular words and passages in *Dubliners*. Although on occasion Joyce would agree in despair to major changes in structure or phrasing, his general strategy was an intransigent defense of the placing of every word. Early in the struggle to get *Dubliners* printed he made this comment on the use of the word "bloody" in three stories: "The first passage I could alter. The second passage (with infinite regret) I could alter by omitting the word simply. But the third passage I absolutely could not alter. Read *The Boarding-House* yourself and tell me frankly what you think. The word, the exact expression I have used, is in my opinion the one expression in the English language which can create on the reader the effect which I wish to create." [1] Later Joyce agreed to the deletion of a few more "objectionable" words, but with this warning: "I will not conceal from you that I think I have injured these stories by these deletions." [2] At one point he even considered omitting "Two Gallants," but with the knowledge that such an omission would be "an almost mortal mutilation of my work." [3]

These remarks, and the many others like them in Joyce's correspondence with reluctant publishers, suggest that the fundamental difficulty he had to surmount was the failure to understand his artistic ideals. To the publishers *Dubliners* appeared as a series of naturalistic sketches, without a controlling form; and this was the reaction of most early critics of the collection. But gradually, as the premises of modern symbolic literature came to be better understood, it was realized that the complex methods of *Ulysses* had been prefigured in *Dubliners*. One might say that we now find the form of *Dubliners* familiar because the course of modern fiction has gone the way of Joyce's art. But there is danger in this complacent assumption, and it is still worth while to begin any study of Joyce's stories with a reminder of the painstaking care with which they were written.

In one of his many letters justifying the style and form of *Dubliners*, Joyce made a comprehensive statement of his artistic aims:

My intention was to write a chapter of the moral history of my country and I chose Dublin for the scene because that city seemed to me the centre of paralysis. I have tried to present it to the indifferent public under four of its aspects: childhood, adolescence, maturity and public life. The stories are arranged in this order. I have written it for the most part in a style of scrupulous meanness and with the conviction that he is a very bold man who dares to alter in the presentment, still more to deform, whatever he has seen and heard. I cannot do any more than this. I cannot alter what I have written.[4]

If we follow the various implications of this statement, testing them against Joyce's actual achievement, we can arrive at a clear understanding of the structural and stylistic methods which produce the extraordinary unity of effects in *Dubliners*

I *The Design of* Dubliners

The most obvious source of unity is the common setting. All the stories are concerned with Dublin life at the turn of the century and are chapters in Joyce's "moral history" of Ireland. Taken together, they present an image of Dublin as the "centre" of spiritual, political, and social paralysis. Joyce once remarked, with *Dubliners* in mind:

I do not think that any writer has yet presented Dublin to the world. It has been a capital of Europe for thousands of years, it is supposed to be the second city of the British Empire and it is nearly three times as big as Venice. Moreover, on account of many circumstances which I cannot detail here, the expression 'Dubliner' seems to me to have some meaning and I doubt whether the same can be said for such words as 'Londoner' and 'Parisian' . . .[5]

For an Irish artist living in the early years of this century, Dublin had the advantage of being a national capital which retained its local identity. The provincialism of Dublin against which Joyce revolted, the lack of cosmopolitan life and "European" standards, held out certain opportunities to the artist. Almost untouched by outside forces, Dublin could epitomize Irish life in a way that London or New York could not epitomize the national lives of England or America. The Dublin of 1904 was not an immense city; it could be known in all its moods by a single person—it was more like an overgrown village—and Joyce was intimately familiar with all aspects of the life of the city. And yet, in spite of its limited size, Dublin embodied the major forces of Irish life. Thus the city provided the ideal setting for Joyce's art, giving him a unified yet manageable world which he could criticize by placing it in a larger perspective.

Joyce's Dublin, like T. S. Eliot's London, is an Unreal City a heap of broken images. But, like Eliot, Joyce defines the paralysis of his Unreal City through contrasts with an imagined city founded upon spiritual and political vitality. Behind the present city of Joyce's stories there always looms the shadow of Dublin as it once was, or as it might be. Beneath the sordid details of contemporary life we constantly discern the outlines of a true community, a living city based on communion among men. Joyce's approach to his materials is not negative, and the same mixture of passionate sympathy and critical detachment which marked his personal attitude toward Ireland may be found in the stories of *Dubliners*. One example should prove my point. In "Ivy Day in the Committee Room" the political and moral paralysis of contemporary Dublin life is exposed through a series of contrasts between the stifling atmosphere of the committee room and the heroic career of Ireland's dead hero, Charles Stewart Parnell, in whose honor the ivy is worn. The hollowness of Mr. Hynes's memorial verses becomes obvious when we think of all that the ivy symbolizes. The unrealities of the present have been defined in terms of a remembered reality.

So in *Dubliners* the self-contained world of Dublin itself is one unifying element. Another is the characteristic style. If I had to choose one word to apply to the style of *Dubliners*, that word would be "economy." Nothing is wasted. Every word and every phrase are made to carry their own burdens in the story and in the collection as a whole. Although some of the tales may appear to be slight at first reading, the more the reader examines them the more comprehensive they are seen to be. Joyce relies on implication, on suggestion and symbol, to extend the impact of his tightly constructed scenes. This technique he learned from many sources, but particularly from the French writers Maupassant and Flaubert; indeed, it might be said that *Dubliners* accomplished for English fiction what Flaubert had earlier accomplished for French fiction in his *Trois Contes*. This is surely what Ezra Pound meant in an early review of *Dubliners* when he said: "I can lay down a good piece of French writing and pick up a piece of writing by Mr. Joyce without feeling as if my head were being stuffed through a cushion." [6] In Joyce's hands prose takes on the density and order of poetry, and when we read the stories in *Dubliners* we must exercise the same care in weighing and evaluating each line that we would exercise in the reading of poetry. It was the contrast between the looseness of much Edwardian verse and the tautness of prose such as Joyce's that led Ezra Pound to his famous dictum: "poetry should be written at least as well as prose." [7]

In Joyce's statement of intention he refers to the style of *Dubliners* as one of "scrupulous meanness." Most readers have taken "meanness" as a description of Joyce's unsentimental attitude toward Irish life, and of course they are right. But "meanness" can also signify strict economy, a passion to make the smallest detail carry its full burden. In this sense, "scrupulous meanness" is a perfect description of Joyce's techniques in *Dubliners*. Nothing is ornamental; nothing can be classified as "good description." In his desire to create "epiphanies" of Irish life Joyce has renounced direct commentary in favor of an allusive method in which dialogue and setting express the author's opinions of his characters.

Joyce's control, although constant and sure, is indirect; we as readers must discover the symbolic overtones which expand his brief sketches into significant commentaries upon Irish life. For instance, in "Counterparts" the conflict between the clerk, Farrington, and his immediate superior, Mr. Alleyne, is endowed with political and national overtones by a reference to Alleyne's North of Ireland accent. Suddenly we realize that the struggle between Farrington and Alleyne reflects a national predicament, and that the force behind Alleyne—the employer, Mr. Crosbie—may well represent England. Once the story is viewed in this perspective, Farrington's defeat in the pub by Weathers becomes an emblem of Ireland's national disgrace; and the final scene in Farrington's home—with the little boy crying in fright, "I'll say a *Hail Mary* for you, pa, if you don't beat me"—becomes an epiphany of Ireland's inner corruption. Such an interpretation must be discovered through a close reading of the story's descriptive details, although once grasped it may seem simple and almost inevitable.

"Araby" provides another good example of the manner in which details of description reinforce and extend the total effect of a story. When the small boy enters the already darkening bazaar, the nature of his disillusionment is introduced with this line: "I recognized a silence like that which pervades a church after a service" (45). Taken in isolation, this line would seem to be little more than an evocation of mood; but if we connect it with similar references earlier in the story, a major motif emerges. The home in which the boy lives was once occupied by a priest who left behind a few books, among them *The Abbot* and *The Devout Communicant*. Outside the house the sky is the liturgical color of violet. The boy's love is an idealized love, and he thinks of himself as bearing his chalice "safely through a throng of foes" (41). Like a medieval knight, he will journey to the exotic world of Araby and return with a gift for his lady. He will make a pilgrimage. All these details point toward an association in the boy's mind between his own love and religious devotion, and therefore it is fitting that his final disillusionment should be described with religious overtones. A careful analysis of the last pages of "Araby" shows how the boy's personal despair is extended symbolically until it encompasses religious and political failure. His personal disillusionment is placed in the context of Ireland's general paralysis, and it is our discovery of this enlarged meaning which provides the story's deepest satisfactions.

So far we have been considering the ways in which a common setting and common techniques promote the unity of *Dubliners*. Another source of unity, perhaps the most obvious, is the recurrent themes which bind the stories together. Joyce's statement of intention spells out the central theme: paralysis of the individual spirit and of the community. This theme is announced in the first paragraph of "The Sisters," in the actual paralysis of the old priest; and it is restated in a variety of forms until it reaches its final and most comprehensive treatment in the figure of Gabriel Conroy. But there are many corollaries to this major theme which run through all the stories; one of these is the theme of frustrated escape, which is consistently expressed through contrasts between the drab outlines of Dublin life and the exotic life of some distant land. In "The Sisters" the small boy dreams that the old priest comes to him and tries to confess, as if the boy himself were a priest. The locale of the dream is significant: "I remembered that I had noticed long velvet curtains and a swinging lamp of antique fashion. I felt that I had been very far away, in some land where the customs were strange—in Persia, I thought . . ."(24). Even in his dreams the boy cannot think of himself in a position of authority and spiritual power within Ireland: the dream is set in the distant East.[8]

Once again, in "Araby," the boy's dreams of achievement and fulfilment are associated with the East. The same is true of "Eveline," except in it the escape is not to the East but to the fabulous, distant city of Buenos Aires. And in "The Dead" Gabriel Conroy longs to escape to Europe, to the Continent, in order to free himself from Ireland's provincialism. There is no need to belabor this point. The theme of escape to some distant and exotic haven links together many of the stories; but it is an escape that exists only in reveries, in dreams, and is constantly frustrated by the paralysis of Irish life. The motif of frustrated escape is merely one of many motifs which are repeated and amplified throughout *Dubliners,* and these sustained themes demand that the collection be viewed on one level as a single work.

Turning now from the contributions to unity made by the setting, techniques, and themes of *Dubliners*, let us take a look at the architecture of the collection. The most obvious grouping is suggested by Joyce's statement that he tried to present Dublin "under four of its aspects: childhood, adolescence, maturity and public life":

Childhood	Adolescence	Maturity	Public Life	Epilogue
	Eveline	A Little Cloud	Ivy Day in the Committee Room	
The Sisters	After the Race	Counterparts		The Dead
An Encounter	Two Gallants	Clay	A Mother	
Araby	The Boarding House	A Painful Case	Grace	

"The Sisters," "An Encounter," and "Araby"—all stories of childhood—are told in the first person by a small boy. Embodying many of the experiences of the young Joyce, they allow us to view the moral paralysis of Ireland through the narrow but intense perspective of childhood. Moving on from this group, the next four stories—"Eveline," "After the Race," "Two Gallants," "The Boarding House"—are tales of frustration in adolescence and early manhood. They are followed by four tales of maturity, and three which deal with aspects of public life. The final story, "The Dead," summarizes the major themes of the collection and acts as an epilogue: composed after the other stories had been written and ordered, "The Dead" stands outside Joyce's four-part plan. Thus the collection moves steadily from the perspective of childhood to that of maturity, from the private to the public world. *Dubliners* yields a number of related viewpoints from which we can assess the "paralysis" of Dublin life.

II *"The Sisters"* and *"The Dead"*

Since it is impossible to consider all the stories of *Dubliners* in detail within the limits of this chapter, I shall devote the remainder of my discussion to "The Sisters" and "The Dead," two stories which demand our special attention both because of their individual greatness and because of their crucial positions in the architecture of the collection. In the case of "The Sisters" we possess unique evidence of Joyce's concern with the general form of *Dubliners*. The story was first published separately in 1904, before Joyce had formulated the plan of *Dubliners;* later, when he decided to make "The Sisters" the introductory piece in his collection, Joyce made substantial alterations in the light of his changing artistic aims, and refashioned the story so that it would introduce the important themes of the entire collection.[9]

Joyce's revisions of "The Sisters" may be divided into three categories. First, he shifted the emphasis from the household and the sisters themselves to the little boy. It is easy to see why Joyce made the child the focus of the revised story, since he emphasized by doing so the general movement of *Dubliners* from childhood to maturity. Furthermore, it is appropriate that a moral history of Ireland should open with a young boy's first discoveries of the real nature of his environment.

The second group of changes has to do with the priest's illness. In the first version he is described simply as an "invalid," but in the revised story his malady is specified as "paralysis." This direct reference to the collection's central theme immediately sets the tone of *Dubliners,* and links the opening of "The Sisters" with the closing of "The Dead."

The third group of changes concerns the Catholic Church and the office of the priest. Joyce added the boy's dream, in which the old priest comes as a simoniac to confess. Since a simoniac is one who traffics in religious objects, this addition reinforces the motif of spiritual corruption. But there is another aspect to the dream: the boy regards himself as a kind of priest. This assumption of a priestlike role is confirmed in a later addition, the scene where the boy and his aunt are served sherry and cream-crackers by the sisters. Surely, as Brewster Ghiselin has suggested, the sherry and crackers are meant to remind us of the wine and wafer of Communion. The boy rejects the wafer, the one element offered to the laity in Communion, and takes up the wine, the element reserved for the priest, as if he were sensible of "the great wish" the old priest had for him.[10]

All of Joyce's changes in "The Sisters" were aimed, therefore, at making the story an integral part of the total pattern of *Dubliners*. They emphasize the spiritual paralysis of Dublin and express the young boy's growing awareness that he may one day play a priest-like role—perhaps that of the artist—but only in a foreign land. It is hard to see how anyone, after examining these revisions and additions, could underestimate Joyce's control over his materials, or question the validity of seeing each story as part of a larger design.

Because of its position at the end of the collection, and at the end of Joyce's work on *Dubliners*, "The Dead" brings the themes of all the other stories into vital relationship with each other, while at the same time it traces a complex process of self-recognition which purges *Dubliners* of all vestiges of provincialism. The hero of "The Dead," Gabriel Conroy, bears the name of the archangel who will one day wake the dead. As the story opens, he and his wife, Gretta, come in from the snow and cold of a Dublin winter, into the warmth of the Misses Morkan's annual Christmas dance. Immediately Joyce focuses our attention on Gabriel and begins to characterize him, but not through direct comment; instead, Gabriel is rendered through dialogue and action. He damns himself before our eyes. His first encounter is with the caretaker's daughter, Lily; and his blunder with her reveals his self-centeredness and lack of communion with others. Instead of sympathizing with Lily, Gabriel makes the self-conscious, "generous" gesture: he gives her a coin. The incident has disturbed his pose of self-assurance, and he is convinced that his speech later in the evening will be a failure. Here again his thoughts are controlled by his ego; he feels that he will fail because of his superior education and taste: "He would only make himself ridiculous by quoting poetry to them which they could not understand" (195).

Gabriel now is joined by his wife, and as they joke with the Misses Morkan over Gretta's goloshes, the latest Continental fashion, Gabriel's discontent with Ireland, his longing to escape, is epiphanized. Once he is caught up in the bustle of the dance, Gabriel's confidence begins to return; but again his self-assurance is broken, this time by an encounter with the patriotic Miss Ivors who goads him about his lack of national feeling and his secret intellectual life. She has touched the insecurity and pride revealed earlier in Gabriel's doubts about his speech, and she forces from him the petulant exclamation: "I'm sick of my own country, sick of it!" (206). In contrast to Gabriel's attitude, Gretta longs to return to the west of Ireland where she was born:

"You can go if you like," said Gabriel coldly.
She looked at him for a moment, then turned to Mrs. Malins and said:
"There's a nice husband for you, Mrs. Malins." (208)

At this point in "The Dead" Gabriel, upset and unsure of himself, retires into the embrasure of a window:

Gabriel's warm trembling fingers tapped the cold pane of the window. How cool it must be outside! How pleasant it would be to walk out alone, first along by the river and then through the park! The snow would be lying on the branches of the trees and forming a bright cap on the top of the Wellington Monument. How much more pleasant it would be there than at the supper-table! (208)

At the beginning of "The Dead" the snow seemed to represent— in contrast to the warmth indoors—coldness, isolation, inhumanity. But here, midway through the story, it has been transformed in Gabriel's mind into a symbol of release, of escape and soothing anonymity. Gradually Joyce is preparing us for the complex symbolism of the closing passage.

Once Gabriel is at the dinner table, the conversation turns to great singers; and suddenly the emphasis of the story shifts from the present to the past, to those who are now gone, to the world of the dead. There is talk of monasteries and religious orders, and of monks who sleep in their coffins "to remind them of their last end" (218). Dessert comes just in time, and the exotic fruits from foreign lands bring our thoughts back to the living; it is time for Gabriel to make his speech. Leaning with trembling fingers on the table, he makes a gracious if conventional speech, a speech about change and the inexorable movements of time. But his thoughts are all on his own performance, and signs of emotion in Aunt Kate cause him to hasten nervously to a close. The dinner is over; the guests are ready to depart.

Perhaps this would be an appropriate point at which to pause and review the movement of "The Dead" up to this scene. Gabriel has been placed in a number of revealing situations which emphasize his insecurity and self-love. The theme of change has been introduced, and the world of the dead has been invoked. But all these elements are still in suspension; the remaining action must draw them together and disclose them as aspects of a single, overriding theme.

Cabs come and go outside. Most of the guests are gone. Bartell D'Arcy is singing, and as Gabriel gazes up the staircase from the dark part of the hall he glimpses the still figure of a woman. It is his wife:

She was leaning on the banisters, listening to something. Gabriel was surprised at her stillness and strained his ear to listen also. But he could hear little save the noise of laughter and dispute on the front steps, a few chords struck on the piano and a few notes of a man's voice singing.

He stood still in the gloom of the hall, trying to catch the air that the voice was singing and gazing up at his wife. There was grace and mystery in her attitude as if she were a symbol of something. He asked himself what is a woman standing on the stairs in the shadow, listening to distant music, a symbol of. If he were a painter he would paint her in that attitude. (227)

Gabriel thinks of the scene only as a subject for art. He even constructs a poetic title, "Distant Music," and the music *is* distant to him: it is the music of love and understanding that he has never heard. But for Gretta the music is immediate and overpowering, evoking the memory of Michael Furey, who died for love of her. All Gabriel can see of his wife are the terra-cotta and salmon-pink panels of her skirt. The scene is indeed a "symbol of something," a symbol of Gabriel's separation from Gretta's secret life.

As Gretta and Gabriel drive back to their hotel, Gabriel is inflamed by keen pangs of lust. He thinks of their life together in romantic terms, once more using the phrase "distant music." The imagery of his memories is explicitly sexual: "They were standing on the crowded platform and he was placing a ticket inside the warm palm of her glove. He was standing with her in the cold, looking in through a grated window at a man making bottles in a roaring furnace. It was very cold" (231). Gabriel thinks complacently of the passionate scene he will soon enact, but once they are inside the hotel room Gretta is abstracted and distant. Gabriel, who longs "to be master of her strange mood" (235), tries to impress her with the fact that he loaned a pound to Freddy Malins.

She makes the conventional reply, "You are a very generous person, Gabriel," but we know that Gabriel was not generous; his action was a bid for admiration. In contrast to the generous tears he will soon shed, this praise by Gretta seems intensely ironic.

Gabriel judges that the moment is now propitious for making love, and he begins his advances; but Gretta runs from him and throws herself upon the bed, weeping. First in anger, then in bewilderment, then in humiliation, Gabriel elicits from her the story of Michael Furey. At the end of the confession, he is left alone to confront himself: "She stopped, choking with sobs, and, overcome by emotion, flung herself face downward on the bed, sobbing in the quilt. Gabriel held her hand for a moment longer, irresolutely, and then, shy of intruding on her grief, let it fall gently and walked quietly to the window." (240).

The moment of self-realization, toward which the entire story has been tending, is now upon Gabriel. He suddenly realizes that the secret life he imagined between himself and Gretta was illusory, that his passion was merely self-love. He has never possessed Gretta's soul, never penetrated to the world of self-sacrifice represented by Michael Furey. Here, at the end of "The Dead," at the end of *Dubliners*, Gabriel is given that self-knowledge which is denied to all the other characters except the young boy in "Araby," who sees himself at the close of the tale as a "creature driven and derided by vanity."

But Gabriel's self-knowledge is not the sudden intuition of a child; it is the full experience of a sensitive and intelligent man. Conscious for the first time of his own paralysis, Gabriel rises above his personal limitations and enters into communion with all the living and the dead. For the first time in *Dubliners* there is a true communion, not of the Church but of humanity; and Joyce symbolizes this transformation through the snow, which has been an active agent in "The Dead" from the opening scene. At first the snow seemed to be an emblem of isolation and lack of human warmth; later it became for Gabriel a symbol of soothing, forgetful escape; but finally, at the close of "The Dead," it becomes a complex symbol of Gabriel's new awareness, the impetus which turns his mind away from himself and toward humanity. Tears of true generosity fill his eyes for the first time, and in rhythmic prose which soon takes on the order and intensity of poetry Joyce leaves us with an evocation which balances paralysis against liberation, criticism against sympathy.

Generous tears filled Gabriel's eyes. He had never felt like that himself towards any woman, but he knew that such a feeling must be love. The tears gathered more thickly in his eyes and in the partial darkness he imagined he saw the form of a young man standing under a dripping tree. Other forms were near. His soul had approached that region where dwell the vast hosts of the dead. He was conscious of, but could not apprehend, their wayward and flickering existence. His own identity was fading out into a grey impalpable world: the solid world itself, which these dead had one time reared and lived in, was dissolving and dwindling.

A few light taps upon the pane made him turn to the window. It had begun to snow again. He watched sleepily the flakes, silver and dark, falling obliquely against the lamplight. The time had come for him to set out on his journey westward. Yes, the newspapers were right: snow was general all over Ireland. It was falling on every part of the dark central plain, on the treeless hills, falling softly upon the Bog of Allen and, farther westward, softly falling into the dark mutinous Shannon waves. It was falling, too, upon every part of the lonely churchyard on the hill where Michael Furey lay buried. It lay thickly drifted on the crooked crosses and headstones, on the spears of the little gate, on the barren thorns. His soul swooned slowly as he heard the snow falling faintly through the universe and faintly falling, like the descent of their last end, upon all the living and the dead (241-42).

CHAPTER 4

A Portrait of the
Artist as a Young Man

Joyce said to me once in Zurich:
"Some people who read my book, *A Portrait of the Artist* forget
that it is called *A Portrait of the Artist as a Young Man.*"
He underlined with his voice the last four words of the title.

—Joyce to Frank Budgen[1]

T. S. ELIOT has said that with Joyce, as with Shakespeare,
the "later work must be understood through the earlier, and
the first through the last; it is the whole journey, not any one stage
of it, that assures him his place among the great." [2] This statement
is certainly true; the extraordinary interdependence of Joyce's
works is a major source of their appeal and a sign of their universality. But this interdependence also poses a difficult critical problem. To what extent are we to criticize each work as a self-
sufficient creation, and to what extent should we allow our views
to be qualified by surrounding works?

This problem is particularly acute in the case of *Portrait*, since
the career of Stephen Dedalus is continued in Joyce's next novel,
Ulysses. Obviously we cannot suppress all knowledge of *Ulysses*
when we examine the *Portrait*, and there is some justification for
the theory that the opening chapters of *Ulysses* provide the inevitable conclusion to the structural rhythm begun in *Portrait*. However, I feel that our first duty is to criticize *Portrait* as an autono-
mous work, admitting information from *Ulysses* only when it
supports the clear intention of *Portrait*. Early criticism of *Portrait*
tended toward a romantic identification of Joyce with Stephen
Dedalus, but in a proper reaction to this naïve view many recent
critics have, in my opinion, tended to overemphasize the separation of Joyce and his hero, introducing into *Portrait* the harsher
ironies of *Ulysses*. The burden of this chapter is that Joyce's attitude cannot be classified as romantic identification or aloof criti-

cism, but is a complex blending of the two.[3] In *Portrait*, if not in *Ulysses*, Joyce's view of Stephen resists any easy formulation.

I *The Evolution of* Portrait

When Joyce left Ireland in 1904 for a life of exile, he vowed—like Stephen Dedalus—that he would produce something notable in ten years. *Portrait* is the fulfilment of that vow, and the dateline at the end of the novel ("Dublin, 1904 / Trieste, 1914") strikes a note of triumphant vindication. Actually there is some evidence that Joyce put the finishing touches on *Portrait* early in 1915,[4] but in the dateline he retained the symmetry of his early promise. The gestation of *Portrait* may be dated from January, 1904, shortly before Joyce left Ireland, when he dashed off in one day a short essay entitled "A Portrait of the Artist." [5] The early "Portrait" lies somewhere between fiction and abstract discourse; arrogant in tone, it is not a conventional autobiography but rather an attempt to describe the "individuating rhythm" [6] which links childhood and adolescence with maturity.

The fascinating aspect of this early draft is that Joyce had already sighted, in 1904, the basic rhythm of development which determines the structure of *Portrait*. The hero passes through an adolescent stage of fanatical religious devotion, based upon fear of eternal damnation; but, once he enters the University, his religious faith wanes and he puts on the protective "enigma of a manner." [7] At first the young man thinks he will find in art a form of divine knowledge, but soon his ascetic studies are broken by an awakening to "the beauty of mortal conditions." [8] In a seaside epiphany which was later reworked into the climactic scene of *Portrait*, the hero finds a new inspiration. The vision of a wading girl leads to this lyric cry: "Thou wert sacramental, imprinting thine indelible mark, of very visible grace. A litany must honour thee; Lady of the Apple Trees, Kind Wisdom, Sweet Flower of Dusk." [9] Under the influence of this epiphany the hero goes out to meet the world, isolated and defiant, and the essay ends with an emotional appeal to the audience of the future: "To those multitudes, not as yet in the wombs of humanity but surely engenderable there, he would give the word: Man and woman, out of you comes the nation that is to come . . . amid the general paralysis of an insane society, the confederate will issues in action." [10]

The next stage in the evolution of Joyce's autobiographical novel was the expansion of "A Portrait of the Artist" into *Stephen Hero*, which took place in 1904-6. The fragments of *Stephen Hero* which have survived deal with Stephen's career at University College, and they make engrossing reading for anyone interested in Joyce's artistic development. As the title implies, *Stephen Hero* is much less critical of Stephen Dedalus than is the final *Portrait*. Joyce had not yet achieved perspective on the events of his early life, and the novel is more autobiography than biography.

If we compare the extant portions of *Stephen Hero* with the corresponding sections of *Portrait*, certain drastic changes are immediately apparent. *Stephen Hero* is nearly five times as long as the equivalent section in *Portrait;* Joyce ruthlessly cut *Stephen Hero* when, between 1909 and 1914, he transformed it into *A Portrait of the Artist as a Young Man*. For example, *Stephen Hero* deals at some length with the relationship between Stephen and a girl named Emma Clery; Emma is supplied with a full history, and we are presented with a number of scenes between them. But in *Portrait* Emma Clery is known only by her initials, E—— C——, and Stephen's brief reverie centers around an almost anonymous girl. Similarly, the argument between Stephen and his mother which is fully explored in *Stephen Hero* becomes only a passing allusion in *Portrait:*

> —Cranly, I had an unpleasant quarrel this evening.
> —With your people? Cranly asked.
> —With my mother.
> —About religion?
> —Yes, Stephen answered (508).

These differences between *Stephen Hero* and *Portrait* reflect Joyce's decision to abandon the conventional forms of Realism and to recast his autobiographical novel in the poetic, highly symbolic manner developed in *Dubliners*. But such artistic decisions are always bound up with changes in the writer's point of view, and before we move on to an analysis of *Portrait* itself we will do well to investigate the alterations in Joyce's view of Stephen Dedalus between 1904 and 1914.

Fortunately, as the editors of "A Portrait of the Artist" have noted, there is an incident treated in all three versions which helps us to understand Joyce's shifting conception of Stephen Dedalus.[11]

In the section of the 1904 "Portrait" which describes the hero's youthful religious ecstasy we find this passage: "One day in a wood near Malahide a labourer had marvelled to see a boy of fifteen praying in an ecstasy of Oriental posture. It was indeed a long time before this boy understood the nature of that most marketable goodness which makes it possible to give comfortable assent to propositions without ordering one's life in accordance with them." [12]

Here the incident is used as a straightforward illustration of the boy's extreme devotion, but in *Stephen Hero* it is employed more dramatically. Musing upon Emma Clery's behavior, Stephen compares her conventional religiosity with his own wild behavior. "By all outward signs he was compelled to esteem her holy. But he could not so stultify himself as to misread the gleam in her eyes as holy or to interpret the [motions] rise and fall of her bosom as a movement of a sacred intention. He thought of his own [fervid religiousness] spendthrift religiousness and airs of the cloister, he remembered having astonished a labourer in a wood near Malahide by an ecstasy of oriental posture. . . ." [13]

In both these uses of the incident Joyce does not exploit its inherent irony, but when he came to write the last chapter of *Portrait* he transformed the scene into an example of Stephen's egocentric rudeness. When Cranly is brusque with him Stephen is willing to forgive the rudeness, remembering a like quality in his own behavior: ". . . he remembered an evening when he had dismounted from a borrowed creaking bicycle to pray to God in a wood near Malahide. He had lifted up his arms and spoken in ecstasy to the sombre nave of the trees, knowing that he stood on holy ground and in a holy hour. And when two constabulary men had come into sight round a bend in the gloomy road he had broken off his prayer to whistle loudly an air from the last pantomime" (501). In this passage the original incident has been revised and augmented to fit a new, and more critical, view of the young Stephen. Not only is the material used dramatically, as in *Stephen Hero,* but Joyce has abandoned autobiographical accuracy in order to express his mature vision of the hero's nature. Stephen-Joyce has yielded to a more generalized figure of *the* artist as a young man.

II *Structure*

Turning from the process of composition to the novel itself, I shall examine *Portrait* under three related headings: structure, language, and myth. Since Joyce carefully indicates not only the basic five-part division of the work but the subdivisions within the chapters, it will be useful to have an outline of this structure before us when we consider the "individuating rhythm" of *Portrait* and its relationship to the novel's major themes:

I	II	III	IV	V
First two pages are the work in embryo: Home, Fatherland, Church, response to language	Uncle Charles	Retreat and Confession	Doubt The Director The seaside epiphany: "profane joy"	Doubt again The Dean Esthetics Stephen and Cranly
Stephen at school (Parnell as savior)	Dublin and E—— C——			
	Whitsuntide play: "admit!"			The Diary
Christmas dinner	Visit to Cork			
Stephen's "victory"	Salvation through the flesh			

Portrait opens with a highly compressed section, less than five hundred words in length, which contains the work's leading motifs in embryo. The subjective impressions of early childhood are presented in terms of the five senses, and in language as complex as that of the most difficult modern poetry. We learn of Stephen's artistic nature through his love of music and rhyme; we glimpse his attitude toward father and mother, and through them his future relationship to fatherland and church (Dante's green and maroon brushes). A good deal of Stephen's future life is prefigured in the mesmeric rhyme:

> Pull out his eyes,
> Apologise,

> Apologise,
> Pull out his eyes.
>
> Apologise,
> Pull out his eyes,
> Pull out his eyes,
> Apologise.

Here the boy's faulty sight is coupled with feelings of guilt, and we are introduced to the demand for submission which is repeated like a litany throughout *Portrait*.

After this poetic opening we see Stephen in his first term at school, where the hints of the first section are amplified. Stephen thinks he will die; but instead Parnell, the national hero, dies. Parnell is established as the secular counterpart of Christ, the betrayed savior of Ireland.

Then, in the next section, the magnificent Christmas dinner scene, all the subjective impressions of the first two sections are given dramatic substance. Before the eyes of the terrified child his elders act out the tragic drama of Ireland. This traumatic experience is followed by a return to Clongowes Wood, where Stephen achieves his first triumph: the successful appeal to the rector. Chapter One closes on a note of triumph, and it is only later—when we discover with Stephen that his appeal was treated as a joke—that the hollowness of the triumph is exposed.

Chapter Two opens with Stephen older and the family fortune in decline. In the figure of Uncle Charles we see the "paralysis" of Ireland which threatens to numb Stephen's sensibility. Next we encounter Stephen as a youthful poet: on a page headed by the Jesuit motto he writes a poem to E—— C——, Eileen's successor. Then comes the Whitsuntide play and the half-humorous demand to "admit!"—a demand which reminds Stephen of earlier submissions. This incident is followed by the visit to Cork: while Mr. Dedalus searches the desks in the anatomy theater, Stephen discovers the word "Foetus" cut in the dark wood and begins to brood on the mystery of paternity. The entire scene confirms Stephen's sense of alienation from his father and underlines the stifling nature of his environment. Sick in heart and mind, Stephen is in desperate need of new authority, of some new source of strength; and he feels that salvation may lie in the flesh. Chapter Two ends with his initiation into sexual love.

Chapter Three needs little commentary. Opening with an on-rush of guilt, it is devoted to the soul-searing retreat sermon and Stephen's contrite confession. The ciborium has come to him. He has entered the Communion of the spirit. But as Chapter Four opens, Stephen's new-found faith is wavering. Assailed by doubt and apathy, he rejects the director's offer of a vocation in the priesthood; and, turning from this sterile prospect, he encounters the birdlike girl standing on the seashore. The chapter ends with an epiphany of new life: "Her eyes had called him and his soul had leaped at the call. To live, to err, to fall, to triumph, to recreate life out of life! . . . He felt above him the vast indifferent dome and the calm processes of the heavenly bodies; and the earth beneath him, the earth that had borne him, had taken him to her breast" (432-33).

The effect of this epiphany is short-lived. Chapter Five begins with new doubt and apathy—Stephen feels the drabness of his home and the futility of Irish life pressing in on him from all sides. The conversation with the dean only serves to confirm Stephen's sense of alienation, and in the esthetic discussion with Lynch he presents the articles of his new faith. In *Stephen Hero* we find many of the same esthetic beliefs, and we know from Joyce's notebooks that this was substantially the esthetic theory that he evolved for himself while a student at University College. However, the fact that this was Joyce's own theory in 1900-1904 does not mean that it was still his creed in 1914. We must take the esthetic discussion in *Portrait* as part of the characterization of Stephen—a definition of his state of mind during the final stage of his youthful development.

The esthetic discussion is followed by the conversations between Stephen and Cranly: Cranly sums up in his person all the different figures Stephen has encountered during the course of the novel, and Stephen has the same ambivalent feelings toward Cranly that he has toward Home, Fatherland, and Church. In the conversations with Cranly, Stephen seeks to justify himself and his choice of life; and the novel ends, appropriately, with a series of diary entries that recapitulates Stephen's reasons for choosing "silence, exile, and cunning."

I have rehearsed the action of *Portrait* in this fashion, and at this length, in order to document the underlying rhythm of synthesis and dissolution which determines the novel's structure.

Each chapter builds toward a climax which is an apparent resolution of the tensions dramatized in it. Thus Chapter One ends with Stephen's apparent "victory" in correcting the injustice of Father Dolan; Chapter Two, with the discovery of sensual consolation; Chapter Three, with the release of confession; Chapter Four, with the seaside epiphany; and Chapter Five, with the proud decision to leave Ireland. But in each case the resolution is apparent, not real, and the next chapter destroys whatever triumph Stephen may have achieved.

As Hugh Kenner has observed, "the action of each of the five chapters is really the same action. The pattern of dream nourished in contempt of reality, put into practice, and dashed by reality, is worked out in the five chapters in five main modes, and in numerous subordinate instances." [14] If we look upon the opening episodes of *Ulysses* as a continuation of *Portrait*, this pattern becomes even more symmetrical: Stephen has returned to Dublin to be at the bedside of his dying mother, and the defiant resolutions with which *Portrait* ends are sunk in doubt and apathy. But, as I have indicated earlier, the subordination of *Portrait* to *Ulysses* tends to produce a critical attitude that is insensitive to the fine balance of detachment and sympathy which Joyce maintains throughout *Portrait*.

III *Language*

The complex structural analogies which unify *Portrait* are, in turn, dependent upon a highly charged symbolic language. Joyce's selective method precludes conventional transitions; we are presented with a number of crucial episodes in Stephen's life and are asked to infer the total pattern of his development from these separate episodes. As in T. S. Eliot's *The Waste Land,* the connections and transitions are suggested, not stated. This narrative technique places a much greater burden upon language than the conventional method of *Stephen Hero*. Each episode must be so freighted with symbolic significance that we can judge the whole from the part; the guiding metaphors form the backbone of the novel.

Typical of these guiding metaphors is the novel's complex water imagery.[15] The first reference to water occurs in the fifth paragraph of *Portrait*. "When you wet the bed, first it is warm then it gets cold." Already the image has two potentials, pleasurable and unpleasant. Later at school the word "suck" reminds Stephen of this twin potential: "To remember that and the white look of the lavatory made him feel cold and then hot. There were two cocks that you turned and water came out: cold and hot. He felt cold and then a little hot: and he could see the names printed on the cocks. That was a very queer thing" (250).

Throughout most of Chapter One water has unpleasant associations. The bogwater of the Clongowes baths disgusts Stephen; Wells shoulders him into the "cold and slimy" water of the square ditch. The vision of death comes to him across a sea of waves. But at the end of the chapter, after Stephen's apparent victory over Father Dolan, water suddenly takes on a new and pleasing significance. "The fellows were practising long shies and bowling lobs and slow twisters. In the soft grey silence he could hear the bump of the balls: and from here and from there through the quiet air the sound of the cricket bats: pick, pack, pock, puck: like drops of water in a fountain falling softly in the brimming bowl" (305). As Stephen's state of mind has changed, so have the emotions suggested by water. The final image of drops falling softly into a brimming fountain brings Chapter One to a close on a theme of purification which carries with it overtones of baptism.

Thus in the first chapter of *Portrait* Joyce establishes water as a twin symbol of birth and death. Like Eliot in *The Waste Land*, he is exploiting the ambivalence of our traditional associations with water (drowning and baptism). Depending upon the context, water imagery in the *Portait* may point toward either pleasure or pain, life or death; or it may be used to suggest both at once. Stephen fears the sea since he views it as an emblem of his own futility; but ironically it is the seaside epiphany which awakens him to the demands of life. Toward the end of Chapter Four the water symbolism becomes more subtle, more complex, until all its potentialities are exploited in the final scene of that chapter.

Yet we must remember that the repeated references to water make up only one of many chains of imagery which sew the novel together from the inside. Joyce's descriptive language is charged at every point with symbolic significance, and it is this constant use of symbolism which enables him to convey a full impression of Stephen's development through a few carefully selected episodes. Each episode is not merely an event in Stephen's life, but an epiphany of one aspect of his personality.

Another characteristic of the *Portrait*'s language which should be noted in passing is the manner in which the style changes as Stephen grows toward maturity. Generally speaking, the movement of the novel is from subjective identification with the young Stephen Dedalus to a dramatic presentation of the adolescent artist. In the first chapter Joyce's language almost forces us to identify ourselves with Stephen, yet by the time we reach Chapter Five the style has become so dispassionate that we are able to stand apart from Stephen and judge his actions.

But this general movement from lyrical to dramatic, from subjective to objective treatment, is not the only pattern to be noted. Within this general movement we can discern smaller oscillations between the lyrical and dramatic styles which correspond to those in Stephen's fortune. Each chapter ends on a tone of intense lyricism, corresponding to Stephen's new-found hope; but then—as we move into the next chapter—there is an abrupt change in language which reflects the decline in Stephen's resolution. Thus the splendid lyrical close to Chapter Four, which expresses Stephen's ecstatic acceptance of life, is immediately undercut at the beginning of Chapter Five by the sordid description of Stephen's home. Chapter Four ends with the turning of the tide and a few reflections in distant pools of water—all is serene and calm, the water serving as an emblem of new life. But the next paragraph, which opens Chapter Five, exploits the antithetical value of water: "He drained his third cup of watery tea to the dregs and set to chewing the crusts of fried bread that were scattered near him, staring into the dark pool of the jar. The yellow dripping had been scooped out like a boghole, and the pool under it brought back to his memory the dark turfcoloured water of the bath in Clongowes" (434). Here the tone of the language has been radically changed, the symbolism reversed, and this abrupt reversal emphasizes the change in Stephen's state of mind. *A Portrait of the Artist as a Young Man* owes much of its extraordinary impact to Joyce's precise correlation of action and language.

IV *Myth*

Any consideration of the language of *Portrait* must ultimately lead us to question the implications of the hero's name, and it is at this point that the novel's mythic backdrop obtrudes itself. A *Portrait of the Artist* is, at its deepest reaches, a search for identity; the entire work might be described as Stephen's search for the meaning of his strange name, which contains the secret of his special destiny. We remember how names fascinate the young boy at Clongowes Wood School. We remember that when Stephen first arrives at the school he is asked his name, and when he replies "Stephen Dedalus" Nasty Roche says: "—What kind of a name is that?" (247).

The whole novel explores the meanings of Stephen's name. In the first chapter the lonely child is seeking to locate himself, to discover his own identity: "He turned to the flyleaf of the geography and read what he had written there: himself, his name and where he was" (255). Later Stephen begins to appreciate the mythic overtones of his name. While crossing St. Stephen's Green in Dublin he is reminded of his namesake, the first Christian martyr; obviously Stephen sees himself as a martyred artist, victimized by the uncomprehending Irish. But Joyce makes very little of the associations prompted by his hero's first name, and it is in the implications of the surname "Dedalus" that we find the novel's chief reliance on myth as a controlling device.

According to Greek mythology Daedalus was a fabulous artisan whose name signifies "cunning craftsman." Midway in his career he went to Crete where he constructed the labyrinth in which the monstrous Minotaur was kept. King Minos imprisoned Daedalus and his son Icarus in order to protect the secret of the labyrinth, but Daedalus constructed two pairs of artificial wings which were attached by wax. Using these wings, Daedalus and Icarus escaped from Crete; but Icarus—overcome by youthful pride—flew so near the sun that the wax of his wings melted and he fell to his death in the Aegean Sea.

Joyce insists upon this myth as a background to *Portrait*, both through Stephen's surname and through the novel's epigraph. On the title page of *Portrait* Joyce placed a quotation from the eighth book of Ovid's *Metamorphoses*, which contains the story of Daedalus and Icarus. The line may be translated, "And turned his mind toward unknown arts"; it refers to Daedalus' plan for constructing wings which will defy nature's laws. Here is the entire passage, in Golding's version; the epigraph is the next to last line:

Now in this while 'gan Daedalus a weariness to take
Of living like a banished man and prisoner such a time
In Crete, and longed in his heart to see his native clime.
But seas enclosed him as if he had in prison be;
Then thought he, "Though both sea and land King Minos stop from
 me,
I am assured he cannot stop the air and open sky.
To make my passage that way then my cunning will I try,
Although that Minos like a lord held all the world beside,
Yet doth the air from Minos' yoke for all men free abide."
This said, to unknown arts he bent the force of all his wits
To alter Nature's course by craft . . .

At Stephen's moments of highest decision he thinks of himself as a
direct descendant of his namesake Daedalus, the skilful and crafty
artificer. Typical of these moments is that episode at the end of
Chapter Four when Stephen, walking by the water, hears his
friends calling to him. His name, strangely and significantly distorted by the wind, suddenly takes on an almost mystical meaning:

Now, as never before, his strange name seemed to him a prophecy.
. . . Now, at the name of the fabulous artificer, he seemed to hear
the noise of dim waves and to see a winged form flying above the
waters and slowly climbing the air. What did it mean? Was it a quaint
device opening a page of some medieval book of prophecies and symbols, a hawk-like man flying sunward above the sea, a prophecy of
the end he had been born to serve and had been following through
the mists of childhood and boyhood, a symbol of the artist forging
anew in his workshop out of the sluggish matter of the earth a new
soaring impalpable imperishable being? (429)

And again, at the conclusion of the novel, Stephen's decision to
flee Ireland is accompanied by a prayer to his namesake Daedalus: "Old father, old artificer, stand me now and ever in good
stead." Like Daedalus the fabulous artificer, Stephen hopes to escape his island prison.

But this identification of Stephen with the crafty Daedalus is
not the only possible interpretation of the novel's mythic parallels.
Stephen is the son of Simon Dedalus, and it is certain that Joyce
wishes us to view Stephen as a potential Icarus, destroyed by his

own pride. Even at the moment near the end of Chapter Four when Stephen feels his closest identification with the soaring Daedalus, we are reminded of the fate of Icarus:

His soul was soaring in an air beyond the world and the body he knew was purified in a breath and delivered of incertitude and made radiant and commingled with the element of the spirit. An ecstasy of flight made radiant his eyes and wild his breath and tremulous and wild and radiant his wind-swept limbs.
—One! Two! . . . Look out! [cries a swimmer]
—O, Cripes, I'm drownded! (429)

The bantering cry "O, Cripes, I'm drownded!" casts momentary doubt upon Stephen's ecstatic identification with Daedalus, suggesting that this mood of triumph—like so many previous ones—may soon be dissipated. Stephen is not conscious in *Portrait* of the analogy with Icarus; but we are aware of it, and this awareness buttresses Joyce's irony. However, in *Ulysses* Stephen acknowledges and exploits the irony: "Fabulous artificer, the hawklike man. You flew. Whereto? Newhaven-Dieppe, steerage passenger. Paris and back. Lapwing. Icarus. *Pater, ait.* Seabedabbled, fallen, weltering. Lapwing you are. Lapwing he" (208).

The lapwing is notorious for its erratic flight, and the self-pitying Stephen of *Ulysses* can only see himself as a petty Icarus. But this is simply one *persona,* one mask, replacing another: Joyce's own view subsumes both extremes, and he is able in *Portrait* to give full value to Stephen's aspirations while at the same time exposing their limitations. We see Stephen as a sterile egoist, cut off from humanity by his lonely pride; yet we also appreciate his imaginative powers, and sympathize with his plight. The great triumph of *Portrait* is Joyce's control of this double view, a control which is sustained through the rhythm of the novel's action, the movements of its language, and the presiding myth of Daedalus-Icarus.

CHAPTER 5

Exiles

AT FIRST thought it may seem strange that Joyce should have turned from the writing of highly successful fiction to the composition of a three-act play, but we must remember that he had long been absorbed in the problems of dramatic art. At an early age he participated in amateur theatricals, and while at University College he reacted vigorously against the provincialism of the Irish theater. "Drama and Life" (1900) was the first paper he read before the college's Literary and Historical Society, and "The Day of the Rabblement" (1901) is a bitter attack on the lack of Continental standards in Irish drama.

As we have already noted in Chapter One, the personality and achievements of Ibsen served as models for the youthful Joyce. His first published essay (which appeared in the *Fortnightly Review*, April 1900) was an enthusiastic review of Ibsen's last play, *When We Dead Awaken;* and in the summer of 1900 Joyce wrote a play called *A Brilliant Career* which has not survived, but which, judging from Stanislaus Joyce's account, was an exercise in Ibsen's themes and methods. At this time Joyce was studying Dano-Norwegian in order to dispense with translations, and by March, 1901, he felt secure enough in the language to write his famous letter of homage to Ibsen, a letter which reveals Joyce's deep personal identification with the Norwegian dramatist.[1] This early devotion to Ibsen's work must be kept in mind while we read *Exiles,* but it explains neither the peculiar form of the play nor the place of *Exiles* in Joyce's artistic development. For answers to these problems we must explore the circumstances surrounding the composition of *Exiles.*

Exiles was drafted in the spring of 1914, but in the previous year Joyce had set down a number of working notes for the play, one of which concerns the title: "Why the title *Exiles?* A nation exacts a penance from those who dared to leave her payable on their return. The elder brother in the fable of the Prodigal Son is Robert Hand. The father took the side of the prodigal. This is probably not the way of the world—certainly not in Ireland. . . ." [2] Richard Rowan, the hero of *Exiles,* is a writer whose career parallels that of Joyce himself. The setting of the play is Dublin, and the year is 1912, the same one in which Joyce made his last visit to Ireland accompanied by his wife and children. Like Joyce, Richard has spent nine years in self-imposed exile in Italy, serving his art. Richard has believed, in the words of Stephen Dedalus, that "isolation is the first principle of artistic economy," [3] but now his belief is being put to a crucial test. Now he must justify his actions to himself, to his native land, and to his old friend—and enemy—Robert Hand, the successful journalist who remained in Ireland. Richard must also face the conflict between his love for his wife Bertha ("the earth, dark, formless, mother" [4]) and his attraction toward the spiritual Beatrice, as well as resolve his ambivalent attitude toward Bertha's "freedom" and possible infidelity. The basic dramatic conflict is between that isolation which seems to be the necessity of the artist and that sense of community which alone can supply the materials for his art. Richard's divided mind is clearly expressed in the following exchange with Robert Hand:

RICHARD, *struggling with himself:* I told you that I wished you not to do anything false and secret against me—against our friendship, against her [Bertha]; not to steal her from me craftily, secretly, meanly —in the dark, in the night—you, Robert, my friend.

ROBERT: I know. And it was noble of you.

RICHARD, *looks up at him with a steady gaze:* No. Not noble. Ignoble.

ROBERT, *makes an involuntary gesture:* How? Why?

RICHARD, *looks away again: in a lower voice:* That is what I must tell you too. Because in the very core of my ignoble heart I longed to be betrayed by you and by her—in the dark, in the night—secretly, meanly, craftily. (583)

Exiles is a true problem play, a dialectic without resolution. It is also, I think, an artistic failure; and the causes of this failure deserve scrutiny, since they illuminate much in the nature of Joyce's art.

The failure of *Exiles* as stage drama is not surprising. Joyce's practical experience as a playwright had been scanty, and his early essays reveal that his interest in drama—like that of the Romantic critics—was more the interest of a poet than of a man of the theater. *Exiles* is studded with fine poetic passages, but the awkward stage directions and long "talky" confessions are the mark of unassimilated Ibsen. However, *Exiles* fails even as closet drama, and I think this is because Joyce has not achieved the perspective, the "distancing" of his subject, which marks his treatment of Stephen Dedalus in *Portrait*. Some critics have claimed that Richard Rowan is subjected to a controlled ironic dissection —there has even been the claim that Joyce's clumsy use of Ibsenist devices is ironic—but the play itself will not substantiate these theories.[5] If we are to have sustained irony and parody in *Exiles*, we must import them from *Portrait* and *Ulysses;* the play itself is almost unrelievedly serious, a series of unfocused debates, and we are left with no sense that the characters' problems have been placed in some wider context.

In short, Joyce is too close to his subject. In the long evolution of *Portrait* the experiences of his early life had been processed into a new and objective form, but *Exiles* dealt with later events and attitudes which were still moving on the surface of his mind. We might say that *Exiles* is the *Stephen Hero* of Joyce's middle life, and there is ample evidence to support this theory. The surviving notes for the play are deeply personal, supporting W. Y. Tindall's contention that Joyce himself is the true audience of *Exiles*.[6] The emotions of jealousy probed in the play can with certainty be traced to a crisis which occurred during Joyce's 1909 visit to Dublin, when he was in momentary doubt of his wife's fidelity. Other personal experiences of the 1909-12 period issue in the play's concern with adultery and with the artist's relationship to his native land.[7] The Cornell University Library now holds several manuscript fragments of *Exiles* which differ in many respects from the published drama, and which appear to be parts of Joyce's private copy; in them the connections with his own life are unmistakable.[8] All this evidence suggests that Joyce had not yet attained perspective on the themes of *Exiles*, and that he adopted the dramatic form in order to further a debate within his own mind. The result is a fascinating personal document but an unsuccessful play.

Ezra Pound once said that *Exiles* was "a side-step, necessary katharsis, clearance of mind from continental contemporary thought," [9] and it is certainly true that Joyce exorcised many of his early preoccupations—including his uncritical devotion to Ibsen—through the writing of the play. But the making of *Exiles* was also a catharsis for Joyce of those feelings of jealousy and alienation which plagued his private life, and although the play itself does not surmount them we may assume that the very act of composition freed Joyce of many burdens. It is highly significant that Joyce called a temporary halt to his preliminary work on *Ulysses* in order to finish *Exiles*, since the themes that *Exiles* introduces but fails to control are handled with supreme grace in the great work which occupied the next seven years of his life.

CHAPTER 6

Ulysses

It is an epic of two races (Israelite-Irish) and at the same time the cycle of the human body as well as a little story of a day (life). The character of Ulysses always fascinated me—even when a boy. Imagine, fifteen years ago I started writing it as a short story for *Dubliners!* For seven years I have been working at this book—blast it! It is also a sort of encyclopaedia. My intention is to transpose the myth *sub specie temporis nostri*. Each adventure (that is, every hour, every organ, every art being interconnected and interrelated in the structural scheme of the whole) should not only condition but even create its own technique. Each adventure is so to say one person although it is composed of persons—as Aquinas relates of the angelic hosts.

—Joyce in 1920[1]

ULYSSES is the keystone of Joyce's artistic career, and one of the great achievements of twentieth-century literature. Begun in Trieste and Zurich during the years of World War I, and completed in the postwar Paris of the "Lost Generation," Joyce's epic both embodies and criticizes the chaotic forces of a civilization in transition. The appearance of *Ulysses* and T. S. Eliot's *The Waste Land* in 1922 made that year a decisive turning point in the history of modern European literature. Like *The Waste Land, Ulysses* became a sacred book of the 1920's, influencing the art of many countries; and Joyce found himself a demigod of the cosmopolitan literary world. And yet, although no book was ever less provincial in its conception and execution, the setting of *Ulysses*—as of all Joyce's works—is the Ireland of his youth. By all the complex methods we have come to associate with modern literature, Joyce transformed the parochial Dublin life of 1904 into a universal metaphor. That metaphor is *Ulysses.*

It is impossible to place *Ulysses* in a single well-defined literary tradition, or to assign it to a particular genre. One of Joyce's aims in writing the book was to break down the accepted distinctions between genres and to create a new, unique form out of the resulting confusion. This amalgamation of methods and subjects that were once thought mutually exclusive makes for real difficulty at first reading, and has led to a bewildering variety of critical approaches; but it is a major source of the novel's power. *Ulysses* can be viewed as an encyclopedia of modern life, or a symbolist novel, or a comic extravaganza like *Tristram Shandy*, or a modern *Divine Comedy*, or a stark Naturalistic drama, or even as a conventional novel of character and situation—the list of valid approaches is almost endless. We can only conclude that the best reading of the work is the one which yields the greatest number of related perspectives.

It would be absurd to undertake a thorough analysis of even one episode from *Ulysses* within the limits of this chapter, but it is possible to indicate the ground plan of the novel and some useful critical attitudes. To this end I have divided the chapter into three sections: (1) a brief survey of the characters, action, and major techniques; (2) a detailed analysis of one symbolic motif, designed to illustrate the novel's complex inner harmonies; and (3) a discussion of one major approach to *Ulysses*, that suggested by Joyce's use of the Homeric myth.

I *Structure and Themes*

Ulysses is the story of one day in the life of Dublin. Although hundreds of Dublin's citizens pass through its pages, the action of the novel revolves around the lives of three characters: Stephen Dedalus, Leopold Bloom, and Leopold's wife, Molly. *Ulysses* opens with three episodes devoted to the alienated artist, Stephen, and closes with Molly Bloom's sensuous reverie as she lies in bed waiting for sleep. Within this framework the novel deals primarily with the personality and behavior of its hero, Leopold Bloom.

The Stephen of *Ulysses* is an extension of the Stephen who, at the end of *Portrait*, leaves Ireland to "forge in the smithy of his soul the uncreated conscience of his race." After a brief stay in Paris, he has returned to be at the bedside of his dying mother; and there he has refused her request that he kneel and pray for her. Having rejected family, church, and homeland, Stephen is haunted throughout *Ulysses* by the gnawing remorse of conscience. Although he no longer believes, he cannot escape the influence of his Irish-Catholic heritage: as his companion Buck Mul-

[78]

ligan says, Stephen has the "cursed jesuit strain" in him, "only it's injected the wrong way" (10,8).

Throughout *Ulysses* the mature Joyce preserves a considerable measure of detachment in describing Stephen, the image of his younger self. The irony is heavier than in *Portrait*, the criticism more biting. In his symbolic role Stephen is the type of the introverted artist, separated from society and yet able to judge society by reason of his separation. However, when Joyce deals with Stephen as an individual it is with full realization of his pride and arrogance. No longer the center of Joyce's art, Stephen is often lampooned and caricatured, a process which is carried much further in Joyce's final work, *Finnegans Wake.*

In contrast to the aloof and cold-blooded Stephen, Leopold Bloom is sympathetic, kind, and completely human. It was Joyce's intention to present Bloom "in the round," and we see as many aspects of his personality as possible. No other character in English fiction is surrounded with such a rich array of intimate detail. Whereas Stephen is only the artist, Bloom plays the roles of father and son, husband and citizen.

And yet, in spite of his many roles and complex personality, Bloom is as isolated as Stephen. Within the structure of Irish society he is an outcast, a member of the alien Jewish race. Within the framework of orthodox Hebrew society he is also an outcast, since he has renounced the faith of his fathers. He is even a failure within his own family: the death of his young son Rudy has disrupted Bloom's relations with his wife, and she has turned to a succession of lovers. Bloom's alienation in the realms of national, religious, and family life parallels that of Stephen; throughout the novel both Bloom and Stephen are searching for some feeling of communion to relieve their intolerable isolation. Bloom seeks a substitute for the son he has lost; Stephen, a father to replace the authorities he has rejected. By the end of the novel, and with the help of each other, both have partially succeeded.

Bloom and Stephen are isolated men searching for a community. In contrast to them Mrs. Bloom is stable, self-sufficient, sensuous, having neither vice nor virtue. In one episode (*Ithaca*) Joyce compares her to the earth around which Stephen and Bloom revolve like captured comets. She remains in Bloom's thoughts throughout the day; he returns to her bed at night; and it is to her that Joyce gives the final episode of the novel. In Joyce's own words, she is "sane full amoral fertilisable untrustworthy engaging shrewd limited prudent indifferent."[2]

Since *Ulysses* deals with only one day in the lives of its characters—June 16, 1904, now known in literary circles as "Bloomsday"—how is it possible for Joyce to endow the events of that day with universal significance? The answer is that he has accomplished this remarkable feat by placing the realistic action of the novel in front of a vast symbolic backdrop—by manipulating simultaneously a number of literary and mythic parallels. At one point in *Ulysses* Stephen says: "Every life is many days, day after day. We walk through ourselves, meeting robbers, ghosts, giants, old men, young men, wives, widows, brothers-in-love. But always meeting ourselves" (210, 213). By virtue of the symbolic roles which Joyce has assigned to them, Stephen and Bloom are many men during the course of one day; but they are always meeting themselves, they maintain their identities as individuals, and Joyce seldom allows the symbolic action to obscure the naturalistic setting.

An example of this manipulation of symbolic correspondences may be seen in the frequent allusions to Shakespeare's *Hamlet*. There are references in every episode, and one entire section (the Library episode) is devoted to a discussion of Shakespeare's life and art. To amplify his treatment of Stephen as son and Bloom as father, Joyce tentatively identifies Stephen with Hamlet, Prince of Denmark, and Bloom with the ghost of Hamlet's father. These associations greatly enrich the texture of the novel and help to define Stephen's attitude: the ambivalence of Hamlet's feeling for the ghost is a correlative for Stephen's uncertain attitude toward the home, church and fatherland that he has rejected.

If the *Hamlet* myth is the primary analogue of Stephen's actions, the Homeric myth indicated by the novel's title is the major symbolic backdrop for Bloom's day in Dublin. Joyce assigned an Homeric tag to each of the eighteen episodes of *Ulysses* (see page 97), and the action of each episode is illuminated by a corresponding section of the *Odyssey*. Bloom is associated with Ulysses, Stephen with Telemachus, Molly with Penelope, and most of the other characters have their Homeric counterparts. As I shall demonstrate later in this chapter, Joyce uses the correspondences with the *Odyssey* to define Bloom's nature and to endow his behavior with general significance. As T. S. Eliot said in an early essay on *Ulysses* (perhaps with his own *Waste Land* in mind):

Ulysses

In using the myth, in manipulating a continuous parallel between contemporaneity and antiquity, Mr. Joyce is pursuing a method which others must pursue after him. . . . It is simply a way of controlling, of ordering, of giving a shape and a significance to the immense panorama of futility and anarchy which is contemporary history. . . . It is a method for which the horoscope is auspicious. Psychology (such as it is, and whether our reaction to it be comic or serious), ethnology, and *The Golden Bough* have concurred to make possible what was impossible even a few years ago. Instead of narrative method, we may now use the mythical method. It is, I seriously believe, a step toward making the modern world possible for art. . . .[3]

In addition to these obvious uses of *Hamlet* and the *Odyssey*, Joyce invented many more structural patterns which give unity to the diversified materials of *Ulysses*. An intricate network of cross-references and recurring motifs binds the eighteen episodes together; furthermore, each episode is unified within itself by the use of a single setting and a distinctive mode of narration, as well as by repeated references to an appropriate art, color, symbol, and organ of the body (see Joyce's *schema* for the novel, reproduced on page 97). For example, the fourteenth episode (*Oxen of the Sun*) takes place in a hospital, where a child is being born. In order to harmonize his form with his subject matter, Joyce makes frequent references to the womb and to the art of medicine, takes the "mother" as his guiding symbol, and narrates the episode according to a technique labeled "embryonic development." The style of the episode changes as the action progresses, and this change reflects *simultaneously* the growth of the human foetus, the geological evolution of the earth, and the development of the English language from Anglo-Saxon to modern slang.[4]

However, all these elaborate ordering devices need not concern the reader during his first encounter with *Ulysses*. They are patterns which helped Joyce to control his materials, and they were more important for him in the making of the novel than they are for us in reading it. Understanding these patterns enriches our appreciation of the novel's central themes, but the patterns themselves are not central. *Ulysses* is primarily concerned with the human and symbolic actions of its major characters.

So far I have presented *Ulysses* as a very serious book, and this is true. However, it is not a sad or a tragic book; it is essentially a comic work, and Joyce's language is the language of comedy. In the Library episode Joyce describes Stephen as laughing "to free his mind from his mind's bondage" (209, 212). The laughter which pervades *Ulysses* is a sign of Joyce's own freedom, the equanimity of his mind and the sureness of his technical control. On his fiftieth birthday Joyce remarked that the adage *in vino veritas* should really be *in riso veritas*, "for nothing so reveals us as our laughter." [5]

The language of this comic epic reflects a desire on Joyce's part to provide each character with a distinctive and characteristic style. We soon learn to recognize Stephen's arid and self-centered prose, or the inquisitive idiom of Mr. Bloom. Much has been made of the "stream-of-consciousness" technique in *Ulysses*, which allows Joyce to record the thoughts and memories as well as the speech of his characters; but in reality the method was employed as early as the mid-eighteenth century by the English novelist Laurence Sterne. However, before *Ulysses* no author had made such extensive use of this method, which attempts to imitate the rambling, associative workings of the mind.

An example of Bloom's "stream of consciousness" is his meditation on the appearance of his friend Martin Cunningham: he associates Cunningham's kind face with that of Shakespeare; Shakespeare brings *Hamlet* to mind; and *Hamlet* suggests suicide. Then his thoughts revert to Cunningham and to Cunningham's drunken wife:

Mr Bloom, about to speak, closed his lips again. Martin Cunningham's large eyes. Looking away now. Sympathetic human man he is. Intelligent. Like Shakespeare's face. Always a good word to say. They have no mercy on that here or infanticide. Refuse christian burial. They used to drive a stake of wood through his heart in the grave. As if it wasn't broken already. Yet sometimes they repent too late. Found in the riverbed clutching rushes. He looked at me. And that awful drunkard of a wife of his. Setting up house for her time after time and then pawning the furniture on him every Saturday almost. Leading him the life of the damned. (95, 96)

In reading a passage such as this one we are reminded of Virginia Woolf's remark that Joyce was "concerned at all costs to reveal the flickerings of that innermost flame which flashes its messages through the brain." [6] As *Ulysses* moved toward comple-

[82]

tion, and Joyce's command of language increased, he tried more and more to make the idioms of the characters mirror their inner natures. In the thirteenth episode, which takes place on the beach, Bloom and a young girl named Gerty MacDowell contemplate each other from a distance and engage in sexual reveries. In terms of style and points of view, the episode divides into two parts: the first part is narrated in the manner of Gerty MacDowell, in the sentimental language of the pulp magazines. Joyce called the style of this part "namby-pamby jammy marmalady drawersy." [7] The last half of the episode, on the other hand, is narrated from Bloom's point of view and is cast in his characteristic idiom. Thus Joyce is able to define the subject of the episode by presenting it from two viewpoints and in two different styles. Here are some passages from the first half of the episode, describing Gerty as she sees herself:

The summer evening had begun to fold the world in its mysterious embrace. Far away in the west the sun was setting and the last glow of all too fleeting day lingered lovingly on sea and strand, on the proud promontory of dear old Howth guarding as ever the waters of the bay, on the weedgrown rocks along Sandymount shore and, last but not least, on the quiet church whence there streamed forth at times upon the stillness the voice of prayer to her who is in her pure radiance a beacon ever to the storm-tossed heart of man, Mary, star of the sea. . . . Gerty MacDowell who was seated near her companions, lost in thought, gazing far away into the distance was in very truth as fair a specimen of winsome Irish girlhood as one could wish to see. She was pronounced beautiful by all who knew her . . . Her figure was slight and graceful, inclining even to fragility . . . The waxen pallor of her face was almost spiritual in its ivorylike purity though her rosebud mouth was a genuine Cupid's bow, Greekly perfect. . . . a telltale flush, delicate as the faintest rosebloom, crept into her cheeks and she looked so lovely in her sweet girlish shyness that of a surety God's fair land of Ireland did not hold her equal. (340-43, 346-49)

Now, for comparison, a fragment of Bloom's interior monologue:

Tight boots? No. She's lame! O!
Mr Bloom watched her as she limped away. Poor girl! That's why she's left on the shelf and the others did a sprint. Thought something

was wrong by the cut of her jib. Jilted beauty. A defect is ten times worse in a woman. But makes them polite. Glad I didn't know it when she was on show. Hot little devil all the same. (361, 367-68)

Perhaps the most impressive example of Joyce's ability to harmonize subject and language occurs in the last episode of *Ulysses*. This section is Molly Bloom's testament, and in it the prose—languid, sensuous, often irrelevant—expresses the mental processes of Mrs. Bloom as she reviews the events of her life and broods on the future. Four key words which are repeated again and again provide the pivots for the episode: these are "he," "bottom," "because," and "Yes." "He" is all Molly's lovers but essentially Bloom, whose image never leaves her mind. "Bottom" emphasizes her sensual nature. "Because" is the principal connective word in her chain of association. And "Yes"—the word which opens and closes the episode—reminds us of Molly's vital, affirmative personality. In the closing lines of *Ulysses*, Molly's memories of her first lover in Gibraltar, of all her lovers, are subsumed in her memory of that day on Howth Hill when she said "Yes" to the proposal of Leopold Bloom:

. . . and O that awful deepdown torrent O and the sea the sea crimson sometimes like fire and the glorious sunsets and the figtrees in the Alameda gardens yes and all the queer little streets and pink and blue and yellow houses and the rosegardens and the jessamine and geraniums and cactuses and Gibraltar as a girl where I was a Flower of the mountain yes when I put the rose in my hair like the Andalusian girls used or shall I wear a red yes and how he kissed me under the Moorish wall and I thought well as well him as another and then I asked him with my eyes to ask again yes and then he asked me would I yes to say yes my mountain flower and first I put my arms around him yes and drew him down to me so he could feel my breasts all perfume yes and his heart was going like mad and yes I said yes I will Yes.

II *Within the Web*

General remarks on the structure and themes of *Ulysses* can serve as rough guides to the novel's difficult terrain, but they are no substitute for local surveys. Only by tracing a single motif through its various metamorphoses can we come to an understanding of the novel's complex laws of development. Like the modern city which it describes, *Ulysses* offers a bewildering variety of routes; but all lead to a few central points. Although the realistic action moves in time through a single day, the movements of the characters' minds follow no temporal sequence but are determined by associational psychology. Only the events of June 16, 1904, are given in chronological order. All the elements provided by memory or association come to the reader piecemeal, and must be ordered in retrospect. Thus, as Joseph Frank says, "Joyce cannot be read—he can only be re-read":

> A knowledge of the whole is essential to an understanding of any part; but . . . such knowledge can be obtained only after the book has been read and all the references fitted into their proper place and grasped as a unity. Although the burdens placed on the reader by this method of composition may seem insuperable, the fact remains that Joyce, in his unbelievably laborious fragmentation of narrative structure, proceeded on the assumption that a unified spatial apprehension of the work would ultimately be possible.[8]

The burden placed on the reader by this method is great, but not insuperable, and the ultimate reward justifies Joyce's demands. For the experienced reader of *Ulysses* the novel exists as a vast web of correspondences, each thread leading to the center of the design. In order to demonstrate this inner harmony of *Ulysses* I shall trace the evolution of a single motif, that of the Isle of Man, showing how it leads the reader to some of the novel's major concerns by way of Manx history, a passage from Matthew, a familiar religious emblem, the Sicily of the *Odyssey*, a seventeenth-century English divine, and a Renaissance notion of unity.

On the way to Paddy Dignam's funeral, the carriage in which Mr. Bloom is riding passes the figure of Reuben J. Dodd, solicitor and moneylender, who later appears in the *Circe* episode as Iscariot and Reuben J. Antichrist. Bloom, in spite of frequent interruptions from Martin Cunningham, tells the story of Reuben's son and the Isle of Man:"—There was a girl in the case, Mr. Bloom began, and he [Reuben] determined to send him to the isle of Man out of harm's way . . ." (93, 94). But on the quay where the boat to the Isle of Man docks, Reuben's son dived into the river Liffey and was fished out by a boatman "more dead than alive." Rather than be sent away from love and into isolation by his father, the son tried to drown himself in the waters of life. Already,

on its first appearance in *Ulysses*, the Isle of Man has been established as a symbol of separation from humanity.

With the introduction of the "House of Key(e)s," the Isle of
Man motif gains in substance (119,120). Bloom's commercial activities in *Ulysses* center around an advertisement for the house of
Alexander Keyes, a tea, wine, and spirit merchant. Keyes has
promised to renew his advertisement in the *Freeman's Journal* on
the condition that the trademark be changed to that recently used
in a Kilkenny paper. This design, a pair of keys crossed near the
top, confronts Bloom throughout the day and is his motive for
visiting the National Library. The crossed keys remind us of St.
Peter's "keys of the kingdom," which are always represented as
crossed; but we must also remember that the lower chamber of
the Manx legislature is called the House of Keys. Bloom has left
the key to his front door at home, Stephen has given the key of the
Martello Tower to Buck Mulligan—and the implications of the
crossed keys make a commentary on this "keyless couple" (652,
668). Their keylessness is, on one level, sexual frustration, for both
lack the "male key" (688, 703) necessary for a satisfactory relationship with women. But it is in the social and spiritual realms—
symbolized by the House of Keys and by the keys of St. Peter—
that their impotence and isolation are greatest.

Bloom, the wandering Jew, thinks of himself as a loyal Irish--
man, but he is rejected by the citizens of Dublin and denied a
feeling of social purpose. Stephen Dedalus has willed his own exile, yet he resents Buck Mulligan as a usurper and longs for some
sense of community. Both Bloom and Stephen are without the key
to the mystery of social living; and, on the broader political level,
all Ireland is keyless too. The Manx people have prospered under
nominal "home rule" since 1866, but in 1904 Ireland is still in political isolation. "When will we have our own house of keys?" cries
Alexander Keyes in the *Circe* episode (480, 489). When Bloom is
proclaimed in his fantasy as the successor to Parnell, and is presented with "the keys of Dublin, crossed on a crimson cushion"
(474, 483), he is fulfilling a dream of political community shared
by the entire nation.

As the emblem of St. Peter, the crossed keys represent the spiritual grace from which Stephen is separated by pride and Bloom
by circumstance:

[86]

Ulysses

And I say also unto thee, That thou art Peter, and upon this rock I will build my church; and the gates of hell shall not prevail against it.

And I will give unto thee the keys of the kingdom of heaven: and whatsoever thou shalt bind on earth shall be bound in heaven: and whatsoever thou shalt loose on earth shall be loosed in heaven.

(Matthew 16: 18-19)

In the *Divine Comedy* (Purg. ix) Peter's keys are placed in the hands of the angel at the Gates of Purgatory; the counterpart in *Ulysses* is the cemetery caretaker in the *Hades* episode who is described as "puzzling two keys at his back" (105, 107). The citizens of *Ulysses* are in hell, and their lack of the keys to social and spiritual communication forms a double image of isolation.

The End of the World occurs in *Ulysses* (495-99, 506-10). Stephen, the son in search of a father, and Bloom, the bereft father looking for a son, are brought together in Bella Cohen's house; but neither is able to assume the role desired by the other. Both are alone, and the immediate failure of their meeting brings to a focus Joyce's criticisms of modern society. The gramophone outside is blaring the "Holy City," Reuben J. Antichrist has safely arrived, and Joyce launches into an eschatological burlesque. The last two verses of the Old Testament are the text for these pages:

Behold, I will send you Elijah the prophet before the coming of the great and dreadful day of the Lord:

And he shall turn the heart of the fathers to the children, and the heart of the children to their fathers, lest I come and smite the earth with a curse. (Malachi 4: 5-6)

The inversion of this passage is complete: Malachi Mulligan is the false prophet; Elijah becomes an American revivalist; and the End of the World is a kilted octopus which *"whirls through the murk, head over heels, in the form of the Three Legs of Man"* (496, 507).

Now the "Three Legs of Man" is the insignia of the Isle of Man (three flexed legs joined at the thighs), and as such it restates the theme of social and spiritual fragmentation. Brought from Sicily by the Vikings, the emblem is a sun symbol.[9] Joyce took Sicily to be the actual setting of Ulysses' encounter with the Oxen of the Sun; it will be remembered that Ulysses' crew, in spite of a solemn warning, slaughtered the cattle of the sun god and were destroyed by a thunderbolt, Ulysses alone surviving because he did not participate in the sacrilege. Joyce interpreted the oxen as fertility symbols, the crime committed against them being one against fecundity; and in the *Oxen of the Sun* episode of *Ulysses* the Homeric crime becomes an analogue for modern sins against nature.[10] The episode in *Ulysses* opens with an invocation to the life-giving sun ("Send us, bright one, light one, Horhorn, quickening and wombfruit"), but the conversation in the episode concerns contraception and perversion: Buck Mulligan proposes to set himself up *on an island* as an anonymous Fertiliser and Incubator. Thus the Isle of Man motif merges with other symbols of spiritual and sexual sterility. According to Joyce, the course of Irish history has been from community to isolation, from Isle of Saints to Isle of Man.

But there is another dimension to the motif. One of the characteristics of Joyce's work is that it tends to comment on its own form, and in his repeated references to the Isle of Man Joyce indicates an obscure source book for *Ulysses*. In his *James Joyce and the Making of 'Ulysses'* Frank Budgen records a conversation in which Joyce, speaking of *Ulysses* as an "epic of the human body," said: " 'The only man I know who has attempted the same thing is Phineas Fletcher. But then his *Purple Island* is purely descriptive, a kind of coloured anatomical chart of the human body. In my book the body lives and moves through space and is the home of a full human personality. The words I write are adapted to express first one of its functions then another." [11] Fletcher's physiological allegory, published in 1633, has as its subtitle *The Isle of Man*. The first half of the poem describes the human body in terms of the geography of an island. Fletcher's dull and rather obvious work cannot be taken seriously as a "source" for *Ulysses*, but the fact that Joyce had the *Purple Island* in mind shows his sympathy for the Renaissance view of man as a compendious image of the macrocosm.

We could go much farther, and into more obscure regions, in tracing the implications of Joyce's references to the Isle of Man. But I think even this brief analysis should indicate the density of the novel's analogies. The reader of *Ulysses* who begins by querying the meaning of a single passage is led inevitably to other passages and related motifs, until he soon finds himself confronted with the work's major themes and with the basic assumptions of Joyce's art.

III *The Homeric Background*

The Homeric background of *Ulysses* has provoked more critical controversy than any other dimension of the novel. No reader can ignore the correspondences with the *Odyssey*, since Joyce's sustained manipulation of Classical parallels provides the best evidence of his attitude toward Leopold Bloom and toward the materials of the novel. The fact that the Homeric correspondences have prompted widely divergent interpretations of *Ulysses* should not discourage us. Although some critics have held that the *Odyssey* is used mainly for ironic contrast, and others have insisted that Bloom be viewed at all times as a reincarnation of Homer's hero,[12] opinion in recent years has tended toward a more balanced—and more interesting—interpretation of the Homeric correspondences, based in part upon a new understanding of Joyce's sources.

In Frank Budgen's *James Joyce and the Making of 'Ulysses'* there is a famous passage which helps us to appreciate the attitude Joyce took toward Homer's hero while he was at work on *Ulysses*. Budgen is recalling a conversation he had with Joyce in 1915, while Joyce was drafting the first adventures of Leopold Bloom. Joyce asked Budgen: "Do you know of any complete all-round character presented by any writer?" Budgen suggested Faust or Hamlet, but Joyce rejected them. For him, the only complete man in literature was Ulysses:

He was subjected to many trials, but with wisdom and courage came through them all. Don't forget that he was a war dodger who tried to evade military service by simulating madness. He might never have taken up arms and gone to Troy, but the Greek recruiting sergeant was too clever for him and, while he was ploughing the sands, placed young Telemachus in front of his plough. But once at the war the conscientious objector became a jusqua'auboutist. When the others wanted to abandon the siege he insisted on staying till Troy should fall. . . . And then "—Joyce laughed—" he was the first gentleman in Europe. When he advanced, naked, to meet the young princess he hid from her maidenly eyes the parts that mattered of his brine-soaked, barnacle-encrusted body. He was an inventor too. The tank is his creation. Wooden horse or iron box—it doesn't matter. They are both shells containing armed warriors. . . . I see him [Joyce's Ulysses] from all sides, and therefore he is all-round in the sense of your sculptor's figure. But he is a complete man as well—a good man. At any rate, that is what I intend that he shall be.[13]

This is a characteristically modern view of Homer's hero; I am reminded of Ezra Pound's advice to W. H. D. Rouse, who was at work on a translation of the *Odyssey:*

> As to the character of Odysseus. Anything but the bright little Rollo of *Chamber's Journal* brought up on Sam Smiles. Born un po' misero, don't want to go to war, little runt who finally has to do all the hard work, gets all Don Juan's chances with the ladies and can't really enjoy 'em. Circe, Calypso, Nausicaa. Always some fly in the ointment, last to volunteer on stiff jobs.[14]

Pound's "bright little Rollo" is, of course, the Ulysses of Victorian poetry and Victorian translation, and if Joyce's novel is read with this interpretation of the *Odyssey* in mind the impact is totally ironic. Leopold Bloom cannot measure up to Tennyson's Ulysses. Each age reveals its literary and moral standards through its versions of the *Odyssey,* and if we are to use Homer's epic as a touchstone to *Ulysses* we must use the epic that Joyce had in mind. Indeed, one might say that Joyce did more than any other writer to shape our modern views of the *Odyssey.* The relationship between *Ulysses* and the *Odyssey* is a dynamic one, each work modifying our view of the other.

The question next arises: how did Joyce, in the last decade of the nineteenth century and the first decade of this century, manage to arrive at an interpretation of the *Odyssey* so far removed from the Victorian interpretation? Was he endowed with a new sensibility by the Time Spirit? Did he—in the course of making himself a modern artist—revolt against the Homer of the nineteenth century for the same reasons that he revolted against many of its literary forms? Or did he stumble upon his new view by chance? There are no simple answers to these questions. It was only natural that Joyce's revolt against the language and ethics of the Victorians should have led him to reject the fashionable versions of the *Odyssey.* Revaluation was part of his self-education.

But beyond this factor of an evolving modern sensibility, Joyce's first knowledge of Homer is of crucial importance. For it was Joyce's destiny to be assigned in school, at the age of twelve, an adaptation of the *Odyssey* which could serve—in sharp contrast to most eighteenth- and nineteenth-century versions—as the foundation for a great modern novel. This version was Charles

Lamb's *Adventures of Ulysses* (1808), an abridgment of the *Odyssey* designed specifically for schoolchildren. In his fine book on the history of the Ulysses theme, W. B. Stanford shows that Lamb's *Adventures* was one of the few nineteenth-century versions of the *Odyssey* which presented a realistic, human figure whose actions were susceptible to symbolic or allegorical interpretation. Considering the extreme importance of Lamb's *Adventures* in the development of Joyce's view of the *Odyssey,* the little book deserves our close attention.[15]

The Irish Intermediate Examination syllabus for 1894 set the first seven chapters of Lamb's *Adventures* for close study, and at the end of the year Joyce had to pass an examination on this material. He did rather well on the examination, and while preparing for it he wrote a short essay, now lost, on Ulysses as "My Favourite Hero." Twenty-three years later, while working on his novel, Joyce told a friend that his fascination with the *Odyssey* dated from 1894: "I was twelve years old when we dealt with the Trojan War at school; only the *Odyssey* stuck in my memory. . . . at twelve I liked the mysticism in Ulysses." [16]

The word "mysticism" is the key, for in the Preface to his *Adventures* Lamb says that the main influence on his language and style was one "obsolete version" of the *Odyssey* (identified in a footnote as Chapman's translation)—and W. B. Stanford has demonstrated that Lamb's version properly belongs in the tradition of allegorical or symbolic interpretations which also includes Chapman's version. This tradition virtually disappeared in the eighteenth and nineteenth centuries, only to flourish again in this century in the works of Joyce and Pound and Kazantzakis. Lamb belongs in the company of those artists who have sensed the *Odyssey*'s mythopoetic force. This tendency to allegorize the *Odyssey* began as early as the sixth century before Christ when one critic used allegorical methods to defend Homer against the moralists, explaining that the names of the gods were best understood as representing moral qualities. The tradition was carried on by later Greek commentators, one of whom—in a figure that is pure Joyce —saw Penelope's web as a system of dialectic, the warp being the premise, the woof the conclusions, and her torch the light of Reason. The Neo-Platonists took the adventures of Ulysses as symbols for the vicissitudes of the soul in its journey through life. And so the tradition goes, down through the Middle Ages, through Dante, and terminating in Chapman and other Renaissance artists who saw in Ulysses' adventures emblems of universal human experience.

Lamb's short Preface indicates the nature of his abridgment and its profound impact on Joyce's imagination. Lamb says that "the ground-work of the story is as old as the *Odyssey*, but the moral and the coloring are comparatively modern"—a remark which could be applied with equal effect to Joyce's *Ulysses*. Lamb then goes on to say that "the agents in this tale, besides men and women, are giants, enchanters, sirens: things which denote external force or internal temptations, the twofold danger which a wise fortitude must expect to encounter in its course through the world." This comment is almost a gloss on Joyce's use of the *Odyssey*. Lamb's emphasis on the symbolic nature of Ulysses' voyage, and his insistence that the fabulous agents denote "external force or internal temptations," point up the adaptability of the *Odyssey*, the ease with which it can be given a modern coloring. A symbolic reading of the *Odyssey* makes it possible to locate Homer's hero in modern Dublin. For although the external forces working on Leopold Bloom are often ridiculously trivial in comparison with those surrounding Ulysses, the internal temptations are frequently the same.

Of course, I am not saying that all of Joyce's knowledge of Homer came from Lamb, but it is true that as late as 1922 Joyce was recommending Lamb's *Adventures* as a guide to *Ulysses*.[17] During the gestation period of *Ulysses*—and Joyce was planning a work based on the *Odyssey* as early as 1906—he read widely in commentaries on Homer. Among the writers consulted were Virgil, Dante, Shakespeare, Racine, Fénelon, Samuel Butler, and Victor Bérard. But it is interesting to note that most of the commentaries Joyce consulted gave substance to the ideas and emphasis derived from Lamb. On the one hand, Joyce was fascinated by historical studies which attempted to establish the realistic qualities of Ulysses; on the other, he read widely in works which explored the symbolic or mystical qualities of the *Odyssey*. Thus he studied the work of Bérard, who claimed that the *Odyssey* was based on the log of an actual seafaring Semite; and he also studied Max Müller, who emphasized the mythic qualities of the *Odyssey* and saw Ulysses as a sun god. Both these theories are present in Joyce's novel: when Leopold Bloom, the wandering

Jew, ends his day in the attitude of a slumbering god, he is described as "Darkinbad the Brightdayler" (722, 737).

We are now in a position to appreciate Joyce's double use of the *Odyssey*. The greatness of *Ulysses* resides in the novel's synthesis of scrupulous naturalism and complex symbolism; and these two modes provide the two Homeric perspectives for Mr. Bloom's day in Dublin: (1) The mock-heroic, or ironic, perspective; and (2) the perspective which reveals Bloom as a modern Everyman, a true counterpart to Homer's hero. Of these two perspectives, the mock-heroic is the least important but—unfortunately—the easiest to comprehend: hence its predominance in most critical readings of the novel. This view of Bloom is based upon a literal comparison between his experiences on June 16, 1904, and Ulysses' experiences during the nineteen years of his wanderings. For an example of the mock-heroic, take the marriage bed of Ulysses: in the *Odyssey* this bed is described as immovable, built into a rooted tree, and the secret of its construction is known only to Penelope and Ulysses. In Joyce's novel, by contrast, the family bed is known to a number of Dubliners, and the characteristic of its construction—the jingling brass rings—is a Dublin joke. Moreover, Bloom returns in the evening to find that the bed has been moved. Thus the ironic contrast between the marriage bed in the *Odyssey* and that in *Ulysses* serves to separate Bloom from his Classical counterpart.

The *Cyclops* episode provides another example. A number of chauvinistic Irishmen have been insulting Bloom's race. Bloom defends the Jewish people so stoutly that, when he leaves the pub, the most violent of the Irishmen, the Citizen, hurls a biscuit tin after him. The Homeric correspondence for this action is, of course, Ulysses' flight from the cave of Polyphemous, with the giant hurling enormous boulders at his ship. If we make a literal comparison between the two events, we are immediately struck by the mock-heroic nature of Bloom's adventure.

And so it goes: almost every Homeric correspondence is subject to mock-heroic interpretation. I would be the last to deny that this irony is an essential aspect of the novel, an important device by means of which Joyce measures the present against an heroic ideal. But it would be a grave mistake to emphasize the irony at the expense of the very real similarities between Bloom and Ulysses. A close examination of the interpretations of those critics who make exaggerated claims for the mock-heroic dimension of *Ulysses* usually reveals two mistaken assumptions.

The first assumption is that Homer's hero is a figure of unimpeachable heroism and virtue, a model of human excellence; but we have seen that Joyce did not hold this view, that he regarded Ulysses as a compendium of human virtues and defects, as a "complete man." The second assumption is that all comparisons between Bloom and Ulysses must be literal or external. It is true that when the Homeric correspondences are taken at the level of "external forces," to borrow a phrase from Lamb's Preface, the impact is usually ironic. But when we take a symbolic view of Ulysses' wanderings the characteristics of Homer's hero can also be found in modern Dublin. Bloom's hasty exit from the pub is subject to this double vision. Externally, the contrast between the boulders of Polyphemous and the Citizen's biscuit tin is ironic, and the disparity provokes laughter; but symbolically both attacks are assaults of Prejudice upon Reason, and carry equal weight.

This double vision is neatly schematized in the thirteenth episode (*Nausicaa*), which was discussed earlier in this chapter. The first part of the episode is completely mock-heroic; the little flirt, Gerty MacDowell, is contrasted ironically with the virtuous Princess Nausicaa (Ulysses was washed up naked on the shore where the modest Nausicaa and her maidens were playing ball). But in the second part of the episode the Homeric background is used without irony. When Bloom discovers that Gerty is lame, he feels a kindness and generosity toward her which are equivalent to Ulysses' emotions when confronted with Nausicaa.

One of the most difficult tasks that faced Joyce during the writing of the last sections of *Ulysses* was finding an appropriate parallel in Bloom's life for the bloody slaying of Penelope's suitors. At first Joyce was baffled, but finally he saw his way clear. No literal parallel was needed; he could rely entirely upon symbolic correspondence. When Bloom, at the end of his day, lies in bed and thinks of Molly's lovers one by one, and then dismisses them with the power of his reason, he is accomplishing the symbolic equivalent of Ulysses' bloody revenge. Joyce realized that no external action of Bloom's could be anything but ridiculous or ironic in contrast to Ulysses' decisive act, yet he also saw that within the context of modern life Bloom's rational dismissal of the suitors was equal, in courage and resolution, to Ulysses' mighty act.

The moral I have been pointing is that we must take the external and internal correspondences together, tempering the irony which results from the former with the sincere emotions evoked by the latter. Joyce's *Ulysses* must be seen in a total perspective which includes both of the Homeric perspectives I have been describing. It was part of Joyce's purpose to present Bloom as simultaneously ridiculous and magnificent, comic and heroic. Bloom is comic in that his actions are often cramped and mean when compared with the wide-ranging experience of Ulysses. But Bloom is also magnificent; his inner fortitude and equanimity of mind reveal a kinship with the Classical hero that can never be completely obscured. Judged by any scale of humanistic values, both Bloom and Ulysses are good men.

So far I have tried to demonstrate the importance of the Homeric correspondences in *Ulysses*, but I do not wish to exaggerate their role. Few aspects of a work of art are as significant in fact as they appear to be in discussion, and I would claim that the Homeric framework of *Ulysses* was more important to Joyce during the process of composition than it can ever be to us as we read the novel. Faced with the task of keeping his materials organized and differentiated while he was at work, Joyce had to resort to many relationships and parallels which never found their way into the final version of *Ulysses*. As he accumulated the thousands of memories and allusions which are the building-blocks of the novel, Joyce felt an acute need for frames of reference which could give some order to the partially formed work. The most satisfactory frame of reference proved to be the *Odyssey*. On his manuscript drafts Joyce labeled each episode with the title of a corresponding Homeric adventure; in his notes he often referred to the characters by their Homeric names. Furthermore, on his note-sheets Joyce used many parallels with the *Odyssey* which were not incorporated in the finished novel. It was Joyce's habit to arrange the materials of a particular episode on note-sheets and then to cross out the items in colored pencil as he used them in successive drafts of the episode. On one note-sheet I have counted fifteen picayune correspondences with the *Odyssey*, but only two of these can be located with any certainty in *Ulysses*; the rest remained on the note-sheet, evidence of a pattern which diminished in importance as the novel neared conclusion. And this proportion of discarded correspondences holds good throughout the note-sheets.[18]

In addition to this qualification, we have to say that only a small number of the Homeric correspondences in the finished novel have any major thematic significance. For instance, the Madame Vera Verity who has advised Gerty MacDowell on the use of "eyebrowline" is analogous to the bright-eyed Athena who opens the Nausicaa section of the *Odyssey;* but this piece of ornamental fun is not necessary to an understanding of the significant parallel between Gerty and Nausicaa. These trivial correspondences— which can only be ferreted out by extended research, and which provide little illumination when they are discovered—must be regarded as vestiges of a rage for order and symmetry which pervaded every aspect of Joyce's art. They are embedded in the novel but hardly participate in its life; they are like fragments of a scaffolding which have been left behind in a completed structure. Thus we have two classes of Homeric correspondences. First, a vast number of small parallels which helped Joyce to keep his materials in order but have little direct relationship to the themes of the novel; and second, a smaller number of major correspondences which provide real illumination.

Joyce himself was well aware of the help he received from the Homeric correspondences during the process of composition. He was also aware that his was a mind which needed more patterns and frames of reference than his readers could ever utilize. This explains his reluctance, after the publication of *Ulysses,* to reveal the *schema* or scaffolding which he had constructed while writing the novel.[19] However, he did give copies of the *schema* to a few friends, and it was copied and recopied, falling into the hands of some critics who made coy allusions to it. Finally, in a gesture of self-defense, Joyce authorized his friend Stuart Gilbert to publish part of the *schema* in his study, *James Joyce's "Ulysses."* It is significant that this published version of the *schema* did not include the detailed Homeric correspondences found on the private copies. The accompanying chart is a simplified version of the *schema*:[20]

The publication of this *schema* was a disastrous event in the history of Joyce's reputation. It had a centrifugal effect on criti-

Joyce's Schema for *Ulysses*

HOMERIC TITLES	SCENE	HOUR	ORGAN	ART	COLOR	SYMBOL	TECHNIC
I. Telemachia (Stephen's Adventures)							
1. Telemachus	The Tower	8 A.M.	——	Theology	White, Gold	Heir	Narrative (young)
2. Nestor	The School	10 A.M.	——	History	Brown	Horse	Catechism (personal)
3. Proteus	The Strand	11 A.M.	——	Philology	Green	Tide	Monologue (male)
II. Odyssey (Bloom's Adventures)							
4. Calypso	The House	8 A.M.	Kidney	Economics	Orange	Nymph	Narrative (mature)
5. Lotuseaters	The Bath	10 A.M.	Genitals	Botany, Chemistry	——	Eucharist	Narcissism
6. Hades	The Grave-yard	11 A.M.	Heart	Religion	White, Black	Caretaker	Incubism
7. Eolus	The News-paper	Noon	Lungs	Rhetoric	Red	Editor	Enthymemic
8. Lestrygonians	Lunch	1 P.M.	Esophagus	Architecture	——	Constables	Peristaltic
9. Scylla & Charybdis	Library	2 P.M.	Brain	Literature	——	Stratford, London	Dialectic
10. Wandering Rocks	Streets	3 P.M.	Blood	Mechanics	——	Citizens	Labyrinth
11. Sirens	Concert Room	4 P.M.	Ear	Music	——	Barmaids	Fuga per canonem
12. Cyclops	Tavern	5 P.M.	Muscle	Politics	——	Fenian	Gigantism
13. Nausikaa	The Rocks	8 P.M.	Eye, Nose	Painting	Grey, Blue	Virgin	Tumescence, detumescence
14. Oxen of the Sun	Hospital	10 P.M.	Womb	Medicine	White	Mothers	Embryonic development
15. Circe	Brothel	Midnight	Locomotor apparatus	Magic	——	Whore	Hallucination
III. Nostos (The Return)							
16. Eumeus	Shelter	1 A.M.	Nerves	Navigation	——	Sailors	Narrative (old)
17. Ithaca	House	2 A.M.	Skeleton	Science	——	Comets	Catechism (impersonal)
18. Penelope	Bed	——	Flesh	——	——	Earth	Monologue (female)

cism, turning the attention of readers from the novel's central themes to its peripheral patterns of organization. For some readers, the *schema* took precedence over the novel itself. However, if the *schema* is treated not as a "key" to *Ulysses* but as a simplified work chart it can be extremely useful. The three-part structure and the major Homeric correspondences are indicated by the titles, and the other information may help with the novel's changing symbols and styles. More importantly, the *schema* as a whole is convincing evidence of Joyce's epic intentions. But every theory suggested by the *schema* must be tested against the novel itself.

We have already considered several reasons which prompted Joyce to use the *Odyssey* as a ground plan for his novel, but I have saved the most important reason for the conclusion of this chapter. When Joyce wrote the word "Ulysses" on the title page his hand might well have trembled, for in doing so he was aligning himself with all those great artists who have treated Homer's theme. The only other modern title of similar impact that I can think of is Thomas Mann's *Dr. Faustus*. Joyce's title is a gesture toward tradition, an appeal to authority; it resembles the invocation of the Muse which initiates the traditional epic. Just as Dante felt the need for a Classical authority, Virgil, to guide him through the hell and purgatory of contemporary existence, so Joyce called upon Homer as a guide to the wanderings of his modern hero, Mr. Leopold Bloom.

CHAPTER 7

Finnegans Wake

A hundred cares, a tithe of troubles and is there one who understands me? One in a thousand of years of the nights?
—*Finnegans Wake* (627.14-16)

JOYCE devoted seventeen years of his life to the writing of *Finnegans Wake* (1923-39). These were years of international fame, but they were also years of family tragedy and approaching blindness. And yet, in spite of illness and despair and the doubts of his friends, Joyce never abandoned his fantastically ambitious work. His letters of the period make painful reading, filled as they are with the details of private crises, but one vital theme runs through them all—Joyce's complete dedication to his "Work in Progress." These facts are worth insisting upon, for they guarantee Joyce's intentions: *Finnegans Wake* is a supremely serious work, not an elaborate literary joke or a fashionable experiment.

It is also a supremely rational work. Although Joyce was personally associated in the 1920's with many writers who wished to exploit the irrational aspects of language, he never shared their artistic convictions. His art stands at the opposite extreme from that of Gertrude Stein. One thing we can say with certainty about *Finnegans Wake* is that its language and structure are as logical as those of *Ulysses*.

A careful study of the last episodes of *Ulysses* makes the transition to *Finnegans Wake* somewhat less difficult. As Joyce's work on *Ulysses* neared conclusion he placed more and more emphasis upon symbolic patterns and less upon realistic action, until in the *Ithaca* episode each naturalistic detail becomes a starting point for an elaborate symbolic commentary. This process was intensified many times over in *Finnegans Wake*, where Joyce aimed not so much at encyclopedic coverage as at total inclusiveness. His purpose was to construct a mythology in which any detail of human behavior—past, present, or future—could be related to the

[99]

cycles of history. Thus Joyce was pleased when, after the publication of *Finnegans Wake,* the Russian invasion of Finland seemed to parallel one of its leading motifs.[1] The work's ability to process new material had been confirmed.

Finnegans Wake is certainly the most difficult book in the English language, and it is likely to remain so for some time. Unlike the once "unreadable" *Ulysses,* which has become more comprehensible with the years, *Finnegans Wake* poses unique problems of interpretation. The difficulties in reading *Ulysses* are less now than they were in 1922 partly because of the work of scholars and exegetes, but also because Joyce's techniques and attitudes have helped to shape the modern literary tradition. The man who can read *The Waste Land* with ease can understand *Ulysses,* since both works belong to a central tradition (in fact, Eliot was heavily influenced by *Ulysses* when he wrote *The Waste Land*). These books have created their own audience and, to a certain extent, the criticial principles by which we judge them. But *Finnegans Wake* is an unique achievement; it is unlikely that the combination of talents and limitations which produced the *Wake* will ever occur again. Joyce's esthetic aims in *Finnegans Wake* may not differ greatly from those of some other modern writers, but the scope and character of their execution make the work *sui generis.* Learning to read *Finnegans Wake* intelligently is not the equivalent of learning a new language (the language of the *Wake* is still English), but it takes almost as much time. For those who wish to make the effort several excellent handbooks are available; these are described in the Bibliography. In the present chapter I can only touch on the structure and language of the *Wake,* and raise a few critical problems.

I *The "Charictures in the Drame"*

Finnegans Wake is concerned with an Irish family, the Earwickers, whose experiences are seen as a microcosm of human history. The head of the family, Humphrey Chimpden Earwicker, keeps a tavern in the Dublin suburb of Chapelizod. He is married to a younger woman named Anna, and they have three children: a daughter, Issy (Isabel, Isolde), and twin sons called Shem and Shaun. The events at Earwicker's tavern during a typical day and night early in this century are the naturalistic plot of the *Wake;* however, it would be a grave mistake to think of these events in terms of action and motivation, the psychology of the traditional novel. Joyce has chosen to make each naturalistic detail the center of an expanding spiral of analogies and motifs which leads ultimately to his macrocosmic themes. As a result, the naturalism of *Finnegans Wake* is so deeply buried beneath its symbolism that intelligent readers cannot agree as to what "happens" in the *Wake,* and when.[2] Perhaps the wisest course is to abandon all conventional notions of what is realistic and what is symbolic, since one of Joyce's purposes in *Finnegans Wake* is to convince us that the contemporary life of Chapelizod possesses no more "reality" than the myths and archetypes it evokes.

In the macrocosm of *Finnegans Wake,* Humphrey Chimpden Earwicker becomes the representative of all men in all ages. He is transformed into a multitude of historical and fictional personages, including Adam and Caesar, Oscar Wilde and Humpty Dumpty. In token of his archetypal role he is most often known by his initials, HCE. The letters HCE may be interpreted as Haveth Childers Everywhere (535.34), a title which identifies Humphrey with all fathers and emphasizes his extensions in time and space. At one point Joyce renders the initials as simply "Here Comes Everybody" (32.18). But HCE is more than all men; he blends into the landscape which plays an active role in *Finnegans Wake.* Joyce identifies HCE with all mountains, specifically with Howth Hill which guards Dublin Bay.

HCE's wife, Anna, is the eternal female principle. She is transformed into a host of famous women, including Eve and Cleopatra, Ann Hathaway and Noah's wife. Her archetypal nature may be seen in the full name given to her at one point: Anna Livia Plurabelle. Anna suggests her role as an individual; Plurabelle, her role as many women; and Livia connects her with the life force and with the river Liffey, which runs through Dublin to the sea. "Anna was, Livia is, Plurabelle's to be" (215.24). Just as HCE is identified with all mountains, so ALP is associated with all rivers. Joyce wove more than six hundred river names into one of the chapters describing her (I. viii).

The children of the Earwicker family play equally complex roles. Issy, the type of the temptress, represents the flirtatious—as opposed to the maternal—aspect of woman. The twins symbolize opposed forces, joined eternally through their conflicts. Shaun, the philistine, is the practical but dull man of affairs; he has nothing but contempt for his brother Shem, who is a burlesque figure of the artist. In creating Shem, Joyce returned to the materials of his early life, but the irony of *Ulysses* has been inflated into caricature. In *Finnegans Wake* it is not the artist but the family man, HCE, who claims Joyce's sympathy.

In order to accomplish this merging of so many identities, Joyce had to make use of the random associations, both in personality and language, which are typical of our dreams. In dreams the conventions of time and space no longer exist; personalities flow into each other, figures from past and present become one. *Finnegans Wake* is a "nonday diary," an "allnights newseryreel" (489. 35) written in stylized dream language. It tells of the subconscious life of a Dublin family, while *Ulysses* deals for the most part with the conscious life of Dublin. But before this "night language" is examined, something must be said about the *Wake's* general design.

II *Structure*

The structure of *Finnegans Wake* is cyclic. The work begins in the middle of a sentence and closes with the first half of that sentence. There is literally no beginning and no end to *Finnegans Wake*. This cyclic structure reflects a cyclic view of history. Joyce believed that life was constant flux but that nothing new ever occurred. Instead, the same types of personality, the same archetypal situations, appear over and over again in different guises. When HCE is tempted by two sluts and three soldiers in Phoenix Park, Dublin, he is simply re-enacting the archetypal temptation in the Garden of Eden. Joyce sums up his theme in this fashion: "Teems of times and happy returns. The seim anew. Ordovico or viricordo" (215.22). Here "ordovico" means Vico's order; Joyce is acknowledging his debt to the eighteenth-century Italian philosopher Giambattista Vico, whose cyclic theory of history is the chief authority for the structure of *Finnegans Wake*.

Vico believed that the first phase of history was divine, characterized by the direct participation of the gods in human affairs. This era was followed by an heroic age, and it in turn by the democratic age in which we now live. When the present age has come to an end, there will be an injection of divine energy—symbolized in *Finnegans Wake* by a thunderclap—and the cycle of history will begin again. *Finnegans Wake* is divided into four books which correspond to Vico's four stages of history, and within this major cycle there are a number of structural epicycles.

Joyce also made use of the Viconian four-part cycle as it applies to the life of the individual: the four phases being birth, marriage, death, and resurrection. The hero of the *Wake* is himself a symbol of cyclic rebirth, since in his person the same basic type is reborn again and again. This theme of resurrection or reincarnation gives a clue to both the meaning and the source of the book's title. "Finnegan's Wake" is an old Irish comic song, which tells the story of hod carrier Tim Finnegan, a hard drinker who falls from the top of his ladder one morning and is taken for dead. His friends hold a wake for him, which turns into a brawl; some whiskey is spilled on Finnegan, and suddenly he revives.

> "Och, he revives! See how he raises!"
> And Timothy, jumping up from bed,
> Sez, "Whirl yer liquor around like blazes—
> Souls to the devil! D'ye think I'm dead?" [3]

Joyce obviously saw in this ballad a symbol for his own indestructible hero, who is constantly falling—like Adam or Humpty Dumpty—only to rise again.

But, remembering the individual application of Vico's cycle, we can make a great deal more out of Joyce's title. The word "wake" must be taken in at least three senses. As the wake of a ship, it represents the hero's course through history. As a funeral watch, it stands for the death of the hero. But Joyce's hero never dies, and his death is followed by resurrection: Finn—again—wakes.

III *Language*

Joyce's punning use of the word "wake" in the title provides a good introduction to the language of his "new Irish stew" (190. 09). In order to express the universal nature of his personages, Joyce needed a language which could present several different meanings simultaneously. For a description of the *Wake's* word-deformations I could turn to Freud; but I prefer to use an author much closer to Joyce than Freud. In *Through the Looking-Glass* (Chap. VI) Lewis Carroll has Humpty Dumpty explain the language of dreams, taking as his text the opening lines of the "Jabberwocky" poem: " 'Twas brillig, and the slithy toves/ Did gyre and gimble in the wabe. . . ." "*Slithy*," says Humpty Dumpty, "means 'lithe and slimy.' 'Lithe' is the same as 'active.' You see it's like a portmanteau—there are two meanings packed up into one word."

In *Finnegans Wake* Joyce is constantly using portmanteau words, but he is seldom content with only two meanings. He also makes lavish use of the pun, which merges apparently unrelated elements through a similarity in sound. In the *Wake* Joyce has altered the English language in an effort to make it do the work of music, where a number of related themes can be sounded at once.

It is best to work our way into this strange language by easy stages. First let us take a simple example, a mock "blurb" Joyce wrote for the dust jacket of the *Wake:*

> Buy a book in brown paper
> From Faber & Faber
> To see Annie Liffey trip, tumble and caper.
> Sevensinns in her singthings,
> Plurabells on her prose,
> Seashell ebb music wayriver she flows.[4]

Here Joyce has altered the familiar nursery rhyme to express the nature of his heroine, Anna Livia Plurabelle, while at the same time reminding us of the original meaning. "Sevensinns" recalls ALP's youth as a temptress, the Eve who causes the fall of man. "Singthings" suggests her musical nature, while "Plurabells" gives us her role as many women. And the distortions in the last line emphasize her flowing, riverlike personality, her identification with the Liffey and with all other rivers.

My next example, a much more complex one, is taken from a passage in the *Wake* which concerns the cycles of history: "From quiqui quinet to michemiche chelet and a jambebatiste to a brulo-brulo!" (117.11-12). "Quiqui" stands for the first of Vico's ages, the obscure origins of language in primitive man's first questions ("Who? What?") when faced with natural mysteries. But the word also suggests human infancy, the questioning child; the individual mirrors in his growth the cyclic development of the race.

"Miche" means "to pilfer" or "to skulk"; it is also French for a round loaf of bread, and in French slang it means "bottom." "Pilfer" and "skulk" suggest the Fall, the forbidden fruit, and Adam

Finnegans Wake

and Eve hiding from the Lord. "Skulk" also implies the guilt obsessions of adult life, while "miche" as a loaf of bread suggests man's role as a breadwinner. Furthermore, "michemiche" is reminiscent of "mishe mishe" on the first page of the *Wake,* and this connection illuminates the entire sentence.

Compared with the multiple meanings of "michemiche," "jambebatiste" is relatively simple; the complex activities of adult life all come to one end. "Jambe" and "batiste" present an image of legs covered by cloth—the shrouded body at the wake. Equally final, "brulobrulo" is the hell (Fr. *brûler*) which must precede resurrection. Taken together, the two compound words represent the death and rebirth of every man and every civilization.

Besides outlining the four-part Viconian cycle in its historical and individual phases, this sentence retraces the history of the particular world-view it expresses. "Quinet" is Edgar Quinet, the translator of Herder and student of Vico; "michemiche chelet" is Jules Michelet, another nineteenth-century French historian and a translator of Vico; "jambebatiste" gives us Vico's first name, Giambattista; and "brulobrulo" is Bruno of Nola, "burnt Bruno," whose theory of contraries is important in the *Wake.* Thus a single sentence recapitulates Vico's cycle on two levels (historical and individual) and simultaneously names the chief sources of Joyce's cyclic theory.[5]

The intricacy and compression of this sentence, which are not unusual in *Finnegans Wake,* should indicate the difficultieŝ that confront the reader. To those who would accuse me of "overreading" the sentence, I can only say that the inner logic of the *Wake* makes such close analysis a necessity. Fortunately, most of Joyce's manuscripts have survived, and we can trace many sections through every phase of their development. These early drafts should not be viewed as "skeleton keys" to the book's meaning— the life of the *Wake* lies in the final synthesis of component parts —but they do yield evidence of Joyce's artistic aims and increase our awareness of the *Wake's* complexity. Let us trace the evolution of one passage in the *Anna Livia Plurabelle* section (200.33-201.04) from first draft to final version.[6]

Anna Livia Plurabelle is, in Joyce's words, "a chattering dialogue across the river [Liffey] by two washerwomen who as night falls become a tree and a stone." [7] The washerwomen scrub the dirty linen of HCE's reputation. In the passage we are concerned with they are discussing Anna Livia's "rhyme," a version of the "letter" discussed in I. v. and partially revealed in Book IV. The following passage appears in the first complete draft of *Anna Livia Plurabelle* (autumn, 1923): "And what about the rhyme she made! O that! Tell me that! I'm dying down off my feet until I hear Anna Livia's rhyme. I can see that. I can see you are. How does it go? Listen now. This is the rhyme Anna Livia made"

During the next few months Joyce labored over the text of *Anna Livia,* and by March, 1924, this brief passage had been enriched by a reference to the nineteenth-century Irish poet Denis Florence MacCarthy: "And what about the rhyme she made! O that! Tell me that while I'm lathering hell out of Denis Florence MacCarthy's combies. I'm dying down off my feet until I hear Anna Livia's rhyme! I can see that, I see you are. How does it go? Listen now. Are you listening? Yes, yes! Indeed I am! Listen now. Listen in:"

This version establishes a basic "narrative" which was not substantially altered throughout the complex process of revision. Joyce's first step in writing the *Wake*'s episodes was to sketch in the "narrative" outlines—then, with a fundamental pattern before him, he began to "thicken" the text. The nature of this "thickening" process was usually dictated by the character of the episode's subject, for Joyce aimed to make the form of each episode expressive of its content. Thus in *Anna Livia Plurabelle,* where the heroine is associated with the river Liffey and all the world's rivers, Joyce sought to make his language as "riverlike" as possible. This "expressive" intent can be discerned in our passage by mid-1925: "And what was the wyerye rhyme she made! O that! Tell me that while I'm lathering hell out of Denis Florence MacCarthy's combies. I'm dying down off my iodine feet until I hear Anna Livia's cushingloo! I can see that, I see you are. How does it go? Listen now. Are you listening? Yes, yes! Indeed I am! Listen now. Listen in:"

Here the "rhyme" has become a "wyerye" one, combining "weary" with the names of two rivers, the Wye and the Rye. The "watery" nature of the passage is also strengthened by the insertion of "iodine." These changes reflect Joyce's obsessive desire to transform the language of *Anna Livia Plurabelle* into the language of all rivers. The chief method for accomplishing this intent was the insertion of river names and allusions: there is not a single river name in the first draft of the episode, but the final version contains well over six hundred. The accumulation of these names occurred mainly in the intermediate stages of composition, where the "expressive" intent dominated Joyce's work on the episode.

The tendency of these intermediate revisions is clearly evident in a later (1927-28) version of our passage.

And what was the wyerye rima she made! O that! Tell me the trent of it while I'm lathering hail out of Denis Florence MacCarthy's combies. I'm dying down off my iodine feet until I hear Anna Livia's cushingloo! I can see that, I see you are. How does it tummel? Listen now. Are you listening? Yes, yes! Idneed I am! Tarn your ore ouse. Essonne inne.

By this version "rhyme" has become the Italian "rima"; "hell" has been altered to "hail"; the "Id" has appeared in "indeed"; and two more river names have been introduced: the Trent and the Tummel. More spectacularly, the innocuous ending of the earlier versions ("Listen now. Listen in:") has become "Tarn your ore ouse. Essonne inne." Although the voice of the washerwoman is still audible in this transformed ending ("Turn your ear here. Listen in."), the emphasis is now on the water-allusions—a "tarn," the Ouse rivers of England, the Essonne River of France, the Inn River of central Europe, and the Öre Sound of Denmark ("öre" is also the Danish for "ear," and Joyce originally wrote "ear," only changing it to "ore" when the functional wordplay became evident).

The expressive intent is even more obvious in the 1930 version of the passage:

And what was the wyerye rima she made! Odet! Odet! Tell me the trent of it while I'm lathering hail out of Denis Florence MacCarthy's combies. Rise it, flut ye, pian piena! I'm dying down off my iodine feet until I lerryn Anna Livia's cushingloo! I can see that, I see you are. How does it tummel? Listen now. Are you listening? Yes, yes! Idneed I am! Tarn your ore ouse. Essonne inne.

Here we have three more additions. "Odet! Odet!" fuses the original meaning ("O that!") with "ode," "Odette," and the Oder River. "Rise it, flut ye, pian piena!" combines the Italian word for flood (*piena*), a type of vessel (flute), and a Russian river (the

Piana) with two musical references: the flute, and the Italian *pian piano* ("softly, gently"). "Lerryn" suggests, among other things, the French river Lers. With these additions the second major period of revision came to an end. Joyce's final work on *Anna Livia* was aimed at strengthening the episode's connections with other parts of the *Wake*, and it was to this end that he inserted the following jingle after "Anna Livia's cushingloo" in his last revision of the passage, thus producing the final version found in *Finnegans Wake* (200-201): "that was writ by one and rede by two and trouved by a poule in the parco!"

In this addition the expressive aim is still evident: "poule" is a reminder of "pool," and "parco" suggests the Pardo River of Brazil. However, the main purpose of the insertion is to connect Anna Livia's "rhyme" with the letter which was "writ by one" (ALP), "rede by two" (Shem and Shaun), and found by a hen in the park (FW 93-94, 104 ff.). Joyce's final elaboration of the passage, like most of his late revisions, was part of an attempt to unify the *Wake* by strengthening its internal harmonies.

It should be clear by now that although *Finnegans Wake* is written in a "night language," the organization of that language is almost stupefyingly rational. The relationship between sound and sense in *Finnegans Wake* has been frequently misunderstood, and we often hear the remark that the book cannot be understood unless it is read aloud. This notion is obviously nonsense; *Finnegans Wake* is filled with visual effects, and Joyce's use of sound to reinforce sense—while often masterly—is not revolutionary. Joyce aimed in *Finnegans Wake* at exploiting all the potentialities of language, and onomatopoeia is only one of these. In fact, the famous "set pieces" in the *Wake* (the ending of *Anna Livia Plurabelle,* the close of Book Four) depend much more upon onomatopoeia than the rest of the work, and therefore tend to give a false impression. It is easy to understand how someone who has only listened to Joyce's great recording of the conclusion to *Anna Livia Plurabelle*[8] might think of *Finnegans Wake* as a "tone poem," but a sampling of other passages soon destroys this theory. The analogy with music *is* a key to the form of the *Wake*, but the analogy is best sustained by Joyce's orchestration of motifs, not by the onomatopoeic effects. Joyce has tried to transform words into musical chords; his portmanteau creations sound a number of related themes or motifs simultaneously. *Finnegans Wake* most resembles a musical composition in its use of leitmotivs and orchestrated language.

IV "Was Liffe Worth Leaving?"

All the characteristics of *Finnegans Wake* that we have been discussing raise difficult questions concerning the work's ultimate value, questions which have scarcely been considered—much less answered—by twenty-five years of criticism. Commentary on the *Wake* has tended to fall into two extreme categories: uninformed generalities and uncritical explication. The dilemma is easy to understand. One can hardly discuss the basic value of the *Wake* without saying what the work means, and this requires laborious explication. Every reference or quotation must be surrounded by an explanatory apparatus before the critic can venture the simplest generalization. For the present, the need would seem to be for more "neutral" explications of structure and themes; but at some point in the future the trend of criticism must turn toward basic questions of value. I should like to suggest a few of these.

Does *Finnegans Wake* justify Joyce's deliberate destruction of temporal sequence? In the last chapters of *Ulysses* we see Joyce moving away from the cause-and-effect sequence of conventional narrative, but in *Finnegans Wake* he has gone much farther: he has ignored the consecutive nature of language itself. Not only are we asked, as in *Ulysses,* to hold all the elements of the work in our minds at every point in our reading, but we are required to apprehend the many levels of meaning in each word or passage simultaneously. By breaking down words and compounding them, Joyce overcame what had been considered an insuperable barrier to the imitation of musical form—the linear nature of language. In music we can hear several notes in an instant of time, but conventional language moves in a temporal sequence, word by word. Of course, the connotations and multiple meanings of words produce a certain amount of orchestration, but Joyce was determined to pack as many meanings and overtones as possible into an instant of time. The question is whether his portmanteau units really do communicate their meanings simultaneously after we have gone through the laborious process of exegesis. Do the many levels of meaning coalesce in the imagination as well as in the conscious mind? My own opinion is that Joyce has succeeded in animating a number of passages—but not the entire work.

Another basic question is that of the relationship between local effects and the *Wake's* general design. As we saw in the evolution of the passage from *Anna Livia Plurabelle,* Joyce's method of composition was essentially ornamental, comparable to that of the mosaic worker or the illuminator of a medieval manuscript. Joyce often thought of his work as analogous to the intricate designs of the *Book of Kells,*[9] an early Irish illuminated manuscript of the four gospels in which the simple fragments of text are enveloped by fantastically involved ornamentation. The visual impact of these illuminations in the *Book of Kells* is unified and overwhelming; every detail seems to grow inevitably out of the central motif. But in *Finnegans Wake* the connections between Joyce's general design and the elaborate local expressions of it do not seem so inevitable. Once again language has stubbornly refused to perform the functions of another art. The major patterns of the *Wake* are impressively presented, and many of the particular passages which mirror these cycles are highly unified. But there is a failure in the middle range; many passsages could be moved about in the book, or even deleted entirely, without doing perceptible damage to the total context. For example, the sentence analyzed earlier ("From quiqui . . . brulobrulo!") could be incorporated into almost any section of the *Wake* having to do with the Viconian cycles. Once he had deliberately sacrificed that sense of "inevitability" or "rightness" in the placing of individual units which comes from a consecutive narrative, Joyce was not quite successful in finding a substitute for it.

Of course, all these critical problems lead to the ultimate question of value: is *Finnegans Wake* worth the time and effort one must expend in order to appreciate its form? The answer will always be determined by individual opinion and taste; I can only point out some of the rewards that come from a knowledge of *Finnegans Wake.* First, there are the pleasures of the book itself. The *Wake* is a textbook on the possibilities (and limitations) of language, but it is also—in those sections where Joyce animates his schematic philosophy—extraordinarily moving. When we read the great passages devoted to ALP (196-216) and HCE (532-54), it is as if we are witnessing the creation of a mythology.

A second reward is the light *Finnegans Wake* casts on Joyce's other works. Especially in its handling of autobiographical materials, the *Wake* draws together themes initiated as early as *Cham-*

ber Music and *Dubliners.* If we view Joyce's works as one vast book containing related treatments of the same subject, then *Finnegans Wake* must be taken as the essential last chapter.

But there is a third reward which goes beyond *Finnegans Wake* and beyond Joyce's art. In his last work Joyce carried many of the methods and assumptions of modern literature to their logical extremes, thereby focusing our attention on crucial esthetic problems. Among other things *Finnegans Wake* was the culmination of two generations of *symboliste* experiments, and as such it illuminates much that has happened in our literature during the past fifty years.

CHAPTER 8

Joyce's Achievement

WHEN Joyce's major works first appeared before the public they were usually regarded as revolutionary documents. Most of the early critics, whether perceptive or imperceptive, emphasized Joyce's innovations in form and subject matter, but then neglected to note his central position in the European literary tradition. Depending upon the critic's point of view, Joyce was either a "new writer in a new form" or a "literary Bolshevik" intent upon destroying the respected conventions. Today it is much easier to "place" Joyce's art in relation to the literature of his own and previous ages.

This new perspective on his works is the result partly of our distance from them in time, and partly of the large body of criticism which has grown up around them; but it is also a product of the changes Joyce wrought in our view of the literary tradition. As T. S. Eliot has said, the literary monuments which exist at a certain moment in time "form an ideal order among themselves, which is modified by the introduction of the new (the really new) work of art among them."

The existing order is complete before the new work arrives; for order to persist after the supervention of novelty, the *whole* existing order must be, if ever so slightly, altered; and so the relations, proportions, values of each work of art toward the whole are readjusted; and this is conformity between the old and the new. Whoever has approved this idea of order, of the form of European, of English literature will not find it preposterous that the past should be altered by the present as much as the present is directed by the past.[1]

Joyce's major works provide an ideal demonstration of Eliot's thesis. Not only have we learned to view them in relation to their predecessors, but our view of the past has been subtly altered by Joyce's achievement. Perhaps the best way to assess this achievement is to consider the interaction between his major works and the literary tradition.

The perfect motto for *Dubliners* would be Joseph Conrad's remark, in his Preface to *The Nigger of the Narcissus,* that any work which aspires to the condition of art "should carry its justification in every line." In this dictum Conrad reveals his affinity with the French stylists, and we are reminded of Ezra Pound's assertion that "in *Dubliners,* English prose catches up with Flaubert." Pound goes on to claim that the Imagist movement in modern poetry, with its insistence on "direct treatment of the THING whether subjective or objective, and the use of NO WORD that did not contribute to the presentation," prepared readers for Joyce's close-textured prose.[2]

Pound was right, of course, in emphasizing the impact of *Dubliners* on English prose style; but in retrospect this aspect of Joyce's achievement seems less important than the influence of *Dubliners* on the general form of the short story. We must remember that the short story is a relatively new form, not much more than a hundred years old, and that during the nineteenth century it developed in two directions: the novel-in-miniature, and the poetic tale. Many nineteenth-century short stories are indistinguishable from the novel in form, the only difference being in length and in range. They depend on the logic of character development displayed through action and dialogue. But the "poetic" short story, which found its first spokesman in Edgar Allan Poe, was informed by a different purpose. Founded upon the Romantic exaltation of the lyric moment, it aimed at a "unity of effects" rather than a unity of action. In the hands of Poe and his followers the short story was devoted to a single powerful effect, which depended upon a poetic exploitation of atmosphere and setting.

In *Dubliners,* Joyce bridged this division within the tradition of the English short story. Writing with Continental models in mind, he managed to preserve the "poetic" unity of the short tale while exploring a wide range of human experience. This enlargement of the genre was accomplished mainly through a subtle handling of symbol and motif. Although the short stories in *Dubliners* are constructed with great economy, so that they take on the quality of lyric moments, they are not limited to a single aspect of life. "Araby," for example, is focused on a single intense experience—

the young boy's disillusionment—but this experience is expanded widely on the symbolic level. Even in "The Dead," the most novelistic of the stories, Joyce has organized Gabriel's experience around a few lyric moments; but we learn more about Gabriel and his world than most writers could convey in a lengthy novel. The controlling symbol of the snow, and the repeated motifs of "generosity" and "the dead," universalize Gabriel's moment of recognition. Most importantly, the general form of the collection —with its elaborate correspondences and recurring themes— shows that Joyce had managed to reconcile the lyric aim of the short tale with the more architectural concerns of the novel, and I consider this reconciliation to be his principal achievement in *Dubliners*.

A *Portrait of the Artist as a Young Man* belongs to the tradition of the *Bildungsroman*, the novel of growth and development, which had its origin in the Romantic concern with confession and self-exploration. Beginning with Rousseau's *Confessions* and Goethe's *Wilhelm Meister*, this form tells of the initiation of a young man into the world, and of his search for identity. Since most novels of this type are founded on personal experience, it is not surprising that the hero of the *Bildungsroman* should often be a young man of artistic temperament and talent who is searching for a vocation. The *Bildungsroman* poses the great themes of the individual's relationship to society, and of the self's relationship to its own image.

In some ways, Joyce's *Portrait* is the crucial work in this form. From the earliest novels in the genre down to the *Portrait*'s immediate predecessors (such as Samuel Butler's *Way of All Flesh* and George Moore's *Confessions of a Young Man*), the author of the *Bildungsroman* had been faced with two formidable problems: how to generalize the experiences of an individual, and how to maintain control and perspective on materials which were often close to his deepest personal emotions. In my opinion, Joyce solved both these problems in a fashion which decisively changed the direction of the genre. If *Stephen Hero* is an illustration of the dangers that surround the writer of a *Bildungsroman*, the *Portrait* indicates one avenue of escape. By abandoning the inclusiveness of the traditional *Bildungsroman* and by concentrating on moments in Stephen's life which could be generalized through myth and symbol, Joyce managed to write of the education of the Artist as well as of the individual. Few novels can have provoked so many sympathetic reactions from widely different people in different countries, the burden of which is: "This is true. This happened to me." Of course, most of the great autobiographical novels of the nineteenth century generalize upon the hero's experiences—Dickens' *Great Expectations* is an impressive example—but Joyce adds another dimension. By emphasizing the general rhythm of Stephen's development, and by concentrating on his reactions to central areas of human experience—language, the family, the church—Joyce endowed Stephen with a representative role. Pip, musing over his father's tombstone in *Great Expectations,* and Stephen, puzzling over the enigma of his strange name, are both engaged in a quest for identity; but Joyce's treatment of the quest is more self-consciously "universal" than that of Dickens. This statement does not mean that the *Portrait* is a better novel than *Great Expectations,* only that it is different, and that it opened up new possibilities in the traditional form.

Similarly, Joyce's handling of autobiographical materials revealed new possibilities in the *Bildungsroman.* Through controlled irony and the use of myth, Joyce clearly establishes a separation between author and hero, thus eliminating the need for extended direct comment in the author's voice. This "distancing" of the hero enhances the novel's dramatic impact and guards effectively against that uncertainty of moral judgment which marks so many nineteenth-century autobiographical novels (such as Meredith's *Ordeal of Richard Feverel*). Joyce's precise control over both sympathy and criticism set a standard of objectivity in the treatment of personal experience which subsequent writers have ignored at their peril, and sent the modern reader back to the great autobiographical novels of the nineteenth century with a new understanding of their form and substance.

In 1912, Joyce gave two lectures at the Università Popolare in Trieste on the subject of Realism (*verismo*) and Idealism (*idealismo*) in English literature: the authors he chose to illustrate these extreme positions were Defoe and Blake. The choice of Defoe and Blake, and the portions of the lectures which have survived,[3] tell us a good deal about Joyce's literary ambitions at the time he began work on *Ulysses.* The lecture on Defoe emphasizes the great possibilities of the realistic form. "Shipwrecked on a lonely island with a knife and a pipe in his pocket," Robinson Crusoe

becomes an "architect, carpenter, knife-sharpener, baker, astron-
omer, ship-builder, potter, farmer, saddle-maker, tailor, umbrella-
maker, and clergyman." [4] Defoe strives for universality by exploring the practical capacities of the individual. In contrast, Blake
learned from Swedenborg how to glorify humanity through an
immense system of "correspondences"; he believed that "each moment shorter than a pulse-beat was equivalent in its duration to
six thousand years." [5] Defoe's archetypal figure is Crusoe, the microcosm; Blake's is Albion, the macrocosm.

We know from Frank Budgen that Joyce had read all of Defoe,
and that he called *Robinson Crusoe* "the English Ulysses." [6] It is
easy to see why. Bloom as an isolated Jack-of-all-trades, cast up
on the shore of Dublin, is another Robinson Crusoe. Like Defoe,
Joyce took an obsessive interest in realistic completeness. When
Ulysses was nearly finished he sent the following extraordinary
request to an aunt in Dublin, one of several such requests. "Is it
possible for an ordinary person to climb over the area railings of
no 7 Eccles street, either from the path or the steps, lower himself
down from the lowest part of the railings till his feet are within 2
feet or 3 of the ground and drop unhurt. I saw it done myself but
by a man of rather athletic build. I require this information in
detail in order to determine the wording of a paragraph." [7]

The paragraph was, of course, that in the *Ithaca* episode (652,
668) in which Bloom is described lowering himself "to within two
feet ten inches of the area pavement" and dropping unhurt into
the areaway. The concern with accuracy and naturalistic completeness revealed in this letter goes far beyond any of the conventional demands of realism, and makes a mystique out of verisi-
militude. It is part of Joyce's rage for order.

At the opposite extreme of the esthetic spectrum, *Ulysses* is controlled by "correspondences" as remote as any Blake derived from
Swedenborg. In the *Ithaca* episode, where Joyce displays his most
obsessive passion for realism, the movements of Bloom and Stephen are charted through abstract astronomical symbolism. In my
opinion, the extremes of realism and symbolism are joined in
Joyce's imagination, and have equal validity. *Ulysses* was written
out of an acute sense of social and personal disorder; hence the
many arbitrary orders which crowd its pages. The form of the
novel is not organic, but constructed; it is like an elaborately
wrought vessel into which the fluid associations of life are poured.

[116]

Rather than indicating a divided mind, Joyce's lectures on Blake and Defoe represent a search for unity.

The course of early criticism on *Ulysses* fluctuated between the novel's extremes of form. This tendency toward extremes is especially evident in the early essays of Pound and Eliot, which set the pattern for much subsequent criticism.[8] Both Pound and Eliot had read preliminary versions of the early episodes while these were appearing serially in the *Little Review* (1918-20), but their responses to the finished work differed widely. Pound's interpretation is founded on the novel's inclusive realism; like Flaubert's *Bouvard et Pécuchet, Ulysses* is a vast catharsis of the European mind. Eliot, on the other hand, emphasizes the novel's mythic structure, which provides a new form for expressing and controlling the "immense panorama of futility and anarchy which is contemporary history." Both men seized upon aspects of *Ulysses* which satisfied their own artistic needs, and in doing so they exaggerated these aspects of its form.

Today we are more likely to praise *Ulysses* for its psychological depth and its profound exploration of historical themes. Now that the extremes of realism and symbolism have been charted and explained, they no longer seem to dominate the work; instead, they compose the background for a moving drama of separation and return. If *Ulysses* is, as I believe, the greatest novel of the twentieth century in English, it is so not because of its special qualities, but because it shares the general characteristics of the other masterpieces of English fiction.

And yet there are disturbing signs in *Ulysses*. In spite of the magnificent closing passage, the final episodes strike us as grotesque in some ways, as not in harmony with the earlier episodes. This feeling of disquiet grows when we realize that in the last phase of his work on *Ulysses* Joyce introduced into the earlier episodes a number of patterns which serve only to justify his *schema* (newspaper headlines in *Eolus*, flower imagery in *Lotuseaters*).[9] We feel that as the novel neared completion Joyce lost interest in the psychology of his characters, and became absorbed in the symmetries of his construction. In a sense, he was already writing *Finnegans Wake*.

Joyce brought to the making of *Finnegans Wake* all the resources of modern anthropology and psychology, and a linguistic virtuosity unequaled in the history of English literature. What he did not bring to it was a sense of "felt life" comparable to that which animates *Ulysses*. The story of the last twenty years of Joyce's life is in large measure the story of his work on *Finnegans Wake*, which was intended to be a self-sufficient cosmos creating its own laws of existence; and there is no doubt that Joyce gradually became a prisoner of that cosmos. I have spoken earlier of the triumphs and limitations of *Finnegans Wake*, which force me to conclude that it is a partial failure. Any set of standards that will account for the essential greatness of *Ulysses* must, I feel, find a certain sterility in *Finnegans Wake*. Even the comic spirit which, much more than the elaborate structural patterns, gives the *Wake* its unity, seems to me ultimately self-defeating. In *Ulysses*, parody and satire have direction because they serve a moral vision; but in *Finnegans Wake* they turn in upon themselves and destroy their own foundations.

It is easy to relate *Finnegans Wake* to a number of literary traditions—*symboliste* experiment, the Irish comic heritage, hermetic writing—but these relationships rarely seem vital. The *Wake* illustrates the extreme tendencies of many traditions without enlarging them. Unlike Joyce's other major works, it does not affect our view of the whole literary tradition; it stands outside the mainstream, asking to be judged in terms of itself. One of the *Wake*'s most intelligent readers, James S. Atherton, has claimed that "strong as are the arguments for the solipsistic nature of *Finnegans Wake* they fall to nothing before the liveliness of the book itself." [10] This is a statement of personal taste, and must be respected as such. But to many readers the "liveliness" of the *Wake* does not touch on life with sufficient frequency to compensate for the work's extraordinary demands.

The one tradition which does stand in vital relationship to *Finnegans Wake* is that of Joyce's own art. At the beginning of his work on the *Wake* Joyce kept a notebook (finally published under the title of *Scribbledehobble*[11]) which contained headings for each of his works up to and including the chapters of *Ulysses*. Under these headings Joyce entered fragments left over from these earlier works, verbal parodies, comments on leading themes: the obvious aim was to make one level of *Finnegans Wake* a summing-up of his artistic career. However, as Clive Hart has pointed out,[12] Joyce partially abandoned this aim in favor of "narcissistic self-parody within *Finnegans Wake* itself"—satiric comment on his own "Work in Progress."

But, whatever Joyce's final attitude may have been, the *Scribbledehobble* notebook does emphasize the unity in Joyce's achievement. In his early (1900) essay on *When We Dead Awaken* Joyce remarked that Ibsen "does not repeat himself," [13] and this quality was to become his own goal. So closely related are all his works, and so carefully do they build on each other, that we may fairly view them as parts of a self-supporting tradition. As each work appeared it modified the others, so that—in T. S. Eliot's words—"his later work must be understood through the earlier, and the first through the last." [14] For this reason anyone who wishes to comprehend Joyce's full achievement must devote his critical attention, if not his unqualified admiration, to *Finnegans Wake*.

Notes and References

Chapter One

1. *The Letters of John Keats,* ed. Hyder Rollins (Cambridge, Mass., 1958), II, 67 (letter of Feb. 19, 1819).

2. For examples of this trend see René Wellek and Austin Warren, *Theory of Literature* (New York, 1949), chaps. VII and VIII; also W. K. Wimsatt and M. C. Beardsley, "The Intentional Fallacy," *Sewanee Review,* LIV (Summer, 1946), 468-88.

3. Stanislaus Joyce, *My Brother's Keeper* (New York, 1958), p. vii.

4. Herbert Gorman, *James Joyce* (New York, 1939). For Joyce's relationship with Gorman see Richard Ellmann, *James Joyce* (New York, 1959), especially pp. 644-45, 735-38.

5. For other references to Gorman in *Finnegans Wake,* see Adaline Glasheen, *A Second Census of 'Finnegans Wake'* (Evanston, 1963).

6. Although Joyce refused to confess and take communion when his mother requested him to do so during her last illness, his refusal to pray occurred after she had entered a coma, when a detested uncle ordered James and Stanislaus to kneel (Ellmann, *James Joyce,* pp. 134, 141).

7. A similar scene took place at the Joyce home, Christmas 1891; see Ellmann, *James Joyce,* p. 33.

8. Richard Ellmann, *Yeats: The Man and the Masks* (London, 1949), p. 179.

9. For the circumstances of Parnell's fall and the "mythic" interpretation of it, see Herbert Howarth, *The Irish Writers: Literature and Nationalism, 1880-1940* (New York, 1959), pp. 1-5; also Ellmann, *James Joyce,* pp. 31-33.

10. *The Collected Poems of W. B. Yeats* (New York, 1951), pp. 275-76.

11. *My Brother's Keeper,* p. 46.

12. This epigram, later used by Stephen in *Portrait* (468) and *Ulysses* (579, 595), appears under the heading "Ireland" in a notebook now held by the Cornell University Library [see *The Workshop of Daedalus,* ed. Robert Scholes and Richard M. Kain (Evanston, 1965), p. 100].

13. *The Critical Writings of James Joyce,* ed. Ellsworth Mason and Richard Ellmann (New York, 1959), p. 228.

14. *Critical Writings,* pp. 48-67.

15. *Critical Writings,* p. 48.

16. Ellmann, *James Joyce,* p. 77.

17. *Ibid.,* p. 90.

18. *Ibid.,* p. 92. Joyce's essay was published in tandem with an essay on women's rights by his friend F. J. C. Skeffington, which had also been rejected by the college magazine.

19. *Critical Writings,* pp. 70-72.

20. *Critical Writings,* p. 76.

21. *Critical Writings,* pp. 81-82.

22. This definition of the Classical temper is drawn from *Stephen Hero* (New Directions, 1963), p. 78. The quotations in the previous sentence are from the Mangan essay, pp. 80-82.

23. The Hill of Tara is a site sacred to Irish tradition; Holyhead is the Welsh port through which the traveler passes on his way to England and the Continent. This aphorism appears under the heading "Ireland" in one of Joyce's notebooks now held by the Cornell University Library (*The Workshop of Daedalus,* p. 101), and it is used by Stephen in the *Portrait* (522).

24. Ellmann, *James Joyce,* p. 27.

25. Kevin Sullivan, *Joyce among the Jesuits* (New York, 1958), p. 7. In the following discussion I have relied heavily upon Mr. Sullivan's fine study, occasionally modifying his argument in the light of the new facts presented by Richard Ellmann in his biography.

26. Quoted in Sullivan, pp. 117-18.

27. Ellmann, *James Joyce,* pp. 48-50.

28. *Ibid.,* p. 56.

29. Quoted in Sullivan, p. 74.

30. *Ibid.,* pp. 74-83. Joyce's notes for *Exiles* are first-rate examples of the "Jesuitical" method.

31. Quoted in Sam Hynes, "The Catholicism of James Joyce," *The Commonweal,* LV (February 22, 1952), 489.

32. Quoted in Sullivan, p. 225.

33. Eugene Jolas, "My Friend James Joyce," in *James Joyce: Two Decades of Criticism,* ed. Seon Givens (New York, 1948), p. 8.

34. Quoted in Sullivan, p. 59. For a different expression of the same conviction, see *My Brother's Keeper,* p. 153, where Stanislaus says that "the definition may change, but the sense of service due to something outside himself *sub specie aeternitatis* abides."

Chapter Two

1. Richard Ellmann, *James Joyce*, pp. 335-36. For the biographical background of "The Dead," see pp. 163-65 and Chap. XV.

2. *Ibid.*, p. 464.

3. *Ibid.*, p. 659.

4. *Ibid.*, pp. 84-86, and see Stanislaus Joyce, *My Brother's Keeper*, pp. 85-86, 143.

5. *My Brother's Keeper*, pp. 85-86.

6. Ellmann, *James Joyce*, p. 118.

7. *My Brother's Keeper*, p. 86.

8. Ellmann, *James Joyce*, p. 241. For a partial listing of the musical settings for *Chamber Music*, see John J. Slocum and Herbert Cahoon, *A Bibliography of James Joyce* (New Haven, 1953), Section F.

9. *My Brother's Keeper*, p. 150.

10. *Stephen Hero*, ed. Theodore Spencer (New Directions, 1963), p. 174.

11. Ellmann, *James Joyce*, p. 361.

12. See Ezra Pound's remark on Imagism and *Dubliners*, quoted in Chapter VIII.

13. Ellmann, *James Joyce*, p. 241.

14. *Ibid.*, p. 270.

15. *Ibid*, pp. 315, 318.

16. *Ibid.*, p. 241.

17. For Stanislaus Joyce's comments on the arrangement of *Chamber Music*, see *My Brother's Keeper*, p. 228, and *Chamber Music*, ed. W. Y. Tindall (New York, 1954), p. 44. Professor Tindall provides an illuminating discussion of the various sequences (pp. 41-48, 102-104, and notes to the individual songs).

18. *Letters of James Joyce*, Vol. I, ed. Stuart Gilbert (New York, 1957, 1966), p. 67. Song XIV was literally the "central song" (No. 17) in Joyce's 1905 arrangement.

19. For an interesting analysis of the cycles of development in *Chamber Music*, see James R. Baker, "Joyce's *Chamber Music*: The Exile of the Heart," *Arizona Quarterly*, XV (Winter, 1959), 349-56.

20. All the extant epiphanies have been reprinted, with commentary, in *The Workshop of Daedalus*.

21. *My Brother's Keeper*, p. 124.

22. The epiphanies themselves support this distinction, which is suggested by Stanislaus Joyce in *My Brother's Keeper*, p. 125.

23. *Stephen Hero*, p. 211.

24. *The Workshop of Daedalus*, p. 11.

25. *Ibid.*, p. 40.

26. The original epiphany reads as follows:

Notes and References

[Dublin: in the National Library]
Skeffington—I was sorry to hear of the death of your brother . . . . .
sorry we didn't know in time . . . . . to have been at the fu-
neral . . . . .
Joyce—O, he was very young . . . . . a boy . . . . .
Skeffington—Still . . . . . it hurts . . . .
[*The Workshop of Daedalus*, p. 32.]

27. *Stephen Hero*, pp. 168-69.

28. Most of the relevant articles have been included in two collec-
tions of *Portrait* criticism: *Joyce's 'Portrait': Criticisms and Critiques*,
ed. Thomas E. Connolly (New York, 1962), and *Portraits of an Artist*,
ed. William E. Morris and Clifford A. Nault, Jr. (New York, 1962). Of
special interest are Irene Hendry, "Joyce's Epiphanies," *Sewanee Review*, LIV (July, 1946), 449-67, and Haskell M. Block, "The Critical
Theory of James Joyce," *Journal of Aesthetics and Art Criticism*, VIII
(March, 1950), 172-84.

29. The surviving fragments of the Paris (1903) and Pola (1904)
notebooks, and all the early essays, may be found in *The Critical Writings of James Joyce*, ed. Ellsworth Mason and Richard Ellmann (New
York, 1959).

30. *Critical Writings*, p. 146.

31. Stephen uses Shelley's image in *A Portrait* (479).

32. *Critical Writings*, p. 78.

33. From "The Day of the Rabblement," *Critical Writings*, p. 69.

34. *Critical Writings*, p. 71.

35. From "An Irish Poet," *Critical Writings*, p. 85.

36. From "Ibsen's New Drama," *Critical Writings*, p. 65.

37. From an early sonnet, "To a Friend." The line was used again
in Arnold's Inaugural Lecture at Oxford (later published as "On the
Modern Element in Literature").

38. First used in Arnold's *On Translating Homer*, this motto is repeated at the beginning of "The Function of Criticism at the Present
Time."

39. *Stephen Hero*, pp. 78-79.

40. From the Paris notebook, *Critical Writings*, p. 145.

41. *Stephen Hero*, p. 77.

42. See *Stephen Hero*, pp. 96, 212-13.

43. *Critical Writings*, p. 148.

44. *Stephen Hero*, p. 213.

45. The following discussion is drawn from the Paris notebook, *Critical Writings*, pp. 143-45.

46. *Critical Writings*, pp. 143-44.

47. *Critical Writings*, p. 144.

Chapter Three

1. *Letters of James Joyce,* Vol. II, ed. Richard Ellmann (New York, 1966), p. 136.

2. *Ibid.,* p. 144.

3. *Ibid.,* p. 142.

4. *Ibid.,* p. 134.

5. *Ibid.,* p. 122.

6. "*Dubliners* and Mr James Joyce," in *Literary Essays of Ezra Pound,* ed. T. S. Eliot (London, 1954), p. 399. First published in *The Egoist,* I (July 15, 1914).

7. "The Prose Tradition in Verse," in *Literary Essays,* p. 373. The immediate reference is to Ford Madox Ford, but the entire argument of this essay illuminates Pound's appreciation of Joyce's early fiction.

8. For an extended analysis of the Oriental motif in *Dubliners,* see Brewster Ghiselin, "The Unity of Joyce's *Dubliners,*" *Accent,* XVI (1956), 75-88 and 196-213. Ghiselin's two-part article is a subtle examination of the symbolic patterns in *Dubliners.*

9. For a detailed and illuminating analysis of the revisions in "The Sisters," see Marvin Magalaner, *Time of Apprenticeship: The Fiction of Young James Joyce* (New York, 1959), pp. 73-86. Magalaner prints the entire 1904 version as Appendix C of his study.

10. Ghiselin, p. 197.

Chapter Four

1. Frank Budgen, *James Joyce and the Making of 'Ulysses'* (Bloomington, 1960), p. 60.

2. In *James Joyce: sa vie, son oeuvre, son rayonnement,* ed. Bernard Gheerbrant (Paris, La Hune, 1949).

3. For a cogent criticism of these extreme views, see Robert E. Scholes, "Stephen Dedalus: *Eiron* and *Alazon,*" *Studies in Literature and Language* (University of Texas), III (Spring, 1961), 8-15.

4. Richard Ellmann, *James Joyce,* p. 365.

5. *Ibid.,* pp. 149-52, where the composition and structure of "Portrait" are discussed. The entire essay, along with some notes for *Stephen Hero,* has been edited by Richard M. Kain and Robert E. Scholes [*The Workshop of Daedalus,* pp. 56-74]. Subsequent references are to this text.

6. P. 60.

7. P. 61.

8. P. 65.

9. P. 66.

10. P. 68.

11. P. 60, fn. 2. See also Robert E. Scholes' discussion of the three versions in "Stephen Dedalus: *Eiron* and *Alazon,*" pp. 10-11.

12. P. 60.

13. *Stephen Hero,* p. 156.

14. Hugh Kenner, "The *Portrait* in Perspective," in *James Joyce: Two Decades of Criticism,* ed. Seon Givens (New York, 1948), p. 169.

15. For another discussion of water imagery in *Portrait,* see W. Y. Tindall, *A Reader's Guide to James Joyce* (New York, 1959), pp. 88-89.

Chapter Five

1. For information on Joyce's early interest in drama, and his admiration for Ibsen, see Richard Ellmann, *James Joyce,* pp. 72-82, 89-93. "Drama and Life," "Ibsen's New Drama," and "The Day of the Rabblement" may be found in *The Critical Writings of James Joyce.*

2. *Exiles,* ed. Padraic Colum (New York, 1951), p. 114. This edition contains Joyce's notes for the play.

3. *Stephen Hero,* p. 33.

4. From Joyce's notes for the play (p. 118).

5. For an ironic reading of the play, see Hugh Kenner, "Joyce and Ibsen's Naturalism," *Sewanee Review,* LIX (Winter, 1951), 75-96.

6. W. Y. Tindall, *A Reader's Guide to James Joyce,* p. 115.

7. For the biographical background to *Exiles,* see Ellmann, *James Joyce,* especially pp. 288-90, 326-28.

8. See Robert M. Adams, "Light on Joyce's *Exiles?* A New MS, a Curious Analogue, and Some Speculations," *Studies in Bibliography* (University of Virginia), XVII (1964), 83-105. Professor Adams prints the fragments of dialogue and speculates on their literary and biographical significance.

9. *Literary Essays of Ezra Pound,* ed. T. S. Eliot (London, 1954), pp. 415-16.

Chapter Six

1. *Letters,* Vol. I, pp. 146-47.

2. *Ibid.,* p. 170.

3. T. S. Eliot, *"Ulysses,* Order, and Myth," in *James Joyce: Two Decades of Criticism,* pp. 201-2.

4. For a detailed and ingenious explication of this episode, based on Joyce's own hints, see A. M. Klein, "The Oxen of the Sun," *Here and Now,* I (January, 1949), 28-48.

5. Eugene Jolas, "My Friend James Joyce," in *Two Decades of Criticism,* p. 8.

6. Virginia Woolf, "Modern Fiction," *The Common Reader: First and Second Series* (New York, 1948), p. 214.

7. *Letters,* Vol. I, p. 135.

8. Joseph Frank, "Spatial Form in Modern Literature," in *Critiques*

and Essays in Criticism, ed. R. W. Stallman (New York, 1949), p. 325.

9. A. W. Moore, *A History of the Isle of Man* (London, 1900), pp. 136-37.

10. See *Letters,* Vol. I, pp. 138-39, and Stuart Gilbert, *James Joyce's 'Ulysses',* new ed. (London, 1952), p. 291.

11. Frank Budgen, *James Joyce and the Making of 'Ulysses'* (Bloomington, 1960), p. 21.

12. Typical of these extreme views are Hugh Kenner's *Dublin's Joyce* (Bloomington, 1956), and Richard Ellmann's "Ulysses the Divine Nobody," *Yale Review,* XLVII (Autumn, 1957), 56-71.

13. Budgen, pp. 15-17.

14. *Letters of Ezra Pound,* ed. D. D. Paige (London, 1951), p. 362. Pound to W. H. D. Rouse, April 17, 1935.

15. For information concerning Joyce's reading of Lamb's *Adventures,* and its influence on *Ulysses,* I am indebted to W. B. Stanford's articles in *Envoy,* V (April, 1951), 62-69, and *The Listener,* XLVI (July 19, 1951), 99, 105. Kevin Sullivan has examined Joyce's reading of Lamb in *Joyce among the Jesuits,* pp. 94-98. See also W. B. Stanford's *The Ulysses Theme* (Oxford, 1954), pp. 186-87. Most of my information on the history of the Ulysses theme is drawn from Stanford's brilliant study.

16. Georges Borach, "Conversations with James Joyce," trans. Joseph Prescott, *College English,* XV (March, 1954), 325.

17. *Letters,* Vol. I, p. 193.

18. See my *Art of James Joyce* (New York, 1964), pp. 20-21.

19. For evidence of this reluctance, see the letter in which Joyce forbids the inclusion of the *schema* in the American edition of *Ulysses* [*A James Joyce Miscellany: Second Series,* ed. Marvin Magalaner (Carbondale, 1959), pp. 10-11]. The *schema* is described as a private document "not meant for publication."

20. The *schema* has survived in two major versions: an early version sent to Carlo Linati in 1920 while *Ulysses* was still a work-in-progress, and a later version supplied to Stuart Gilbert and Herbert Gorman after the publication of the novel. Both versions are reproduced in comparative form in Richard Ellmann, *Ulysses on the Liffey* (New York, 1972). My simplified chart is based on the later version; I have made small changes in spelling and format, and have eliminated the column of detailed correspondences.

Chapter Seven

1. Eugene Jolas, "My Friend James Joyce," in *James Joyce: Two Decades of Criticism,* p. 17. The story of "How Buckley Shot the Russian General" is a leading motif in *Finnegans Wake,* having to do with the father–son conflict, and Joyce saw it repeated in current history: "The most curious comment I have received on the book is a symbolical

one from Helsinki, where, as foretold by the prophet, the Finn again wakes, and volunteer Buckleys are hurrying from all sides to shoot that Russian general. . . ."

2. For a detailed and persuasive discussion of the *Wake's* time-scheme and naturalistic plot, see Clive Hart, *Structure and Motif in 'Finnegans Wake'* (London, 1962), pp. 69-82.

3. For the full text of the ballad, see the entry "Finnegan" in Adaline Glasheen, *Second Census of 'Finnegans Wake'* (Evanston, 1963).

4. Ellmann, *James Joyce,* pp. 629-30.

5. For a fuller examination of this sentence in its context, see my *Art of James Joyce,* pp. 59-62.

6. Most of the manuscripts of *Finnegans Wake* are now in the British Museum. The drafts of *Anna Livia Plurabelle* have been edited by Fred H. Higginson [*Anna Livia Plurabelle: The Making of a Chapter* (Minneapolis, 1960)], and I have drawn my quotations from this edition (pp. 29, 38, 49-50, 64, 82).

7. *Letters,* Vol. I, p. 213.

8. Joyce's recording of FW 213-16 is available in the Folkways Series (FP 93).

9. See James S. Atherton, *The Books at the Wake* (New York, 1960), pp. 61-67.

Chapter Eight

1. T. S. Eliot, "Tradition and the Individual Talent," in *Selected Essays* (New York, 1932), p. 5.

2. Ezra Pound, "Past History," *The English Journal,* XXII (May, 1933), 351-52. In the second quotation Pound is repeating the first two principles of the 1912 "Imagist Manifesto."

3. See Ellmann, *James Joyce,* pp. 329-30, for a discussion of these lectures. The surviving portion of the Blake lecture has been reprinted in translation in *The Critical Writings of James Joyce,* pp. 214-22; the partial text of the Defoe lecture has been edited in the original by Ellsworth Mason (*Criticism,* I [1959], 181-89). For an excellent discussion of Blake and Joyce, see Northrop Frye, "Quest and Cycle in *Finnegans Wake*," *The James Joyce Review,* I (February, 1957), 39-47.

4. Ellmann, *James Joyce,* p. 330.

5. *Critical Writings,* p. 222.

6. Budgen, *James Joyce and the Making of 'Ulysses,'* p. 181.

7. *Letters,* Vol. I, p. 175.

8. Ezra Pound, *"Ulysses"* (1922), reprinted in *Literary Essays of Ezra Pound,* ed. T. S. Eliot (London, 1954), pp. 403-9; and "James Joyce et Pécuchet" (1922), translated by Fred Bornhauser in *Shenandoah,* III (Autumn, 1952), 9-20. T. S. Eliot, "*Ulysses,* Order, and Myth" (1923), reprinted in *James Joyce: Two Decades of Criticism,* pp. 198-202.

9. See my *Art of James Joyce,* pp. 7-33.

10. James S. Atherton, *The Books at the Wake,* p. 13.

11. *James Joyce's Scribbledehobble: The Ur-Workbook for 'Finnegans Wake,'* ed. Thomas E. Connolly (Evanston, 1961).

12. Clive Hart, *Structure and Motif in 'Finnegans Wake,'* pp. 42-43.

13. *Critical Writings,* p. 63.

14. From T. S. Eliot's Introductory Message in *James Joyce: sa vie, son oeuvre, son rayonnement* (Paris, 1949).

Selected Bibliography

Primary Sources

In this section I have listed in chronological order the first editions of Joyce's most important works. For a comprehensive study of his publications, see John J. Slocum and Herbert Cahoon, *A Bibliography of James Joyce* (New Haven: Yale University Press, 1953).

"Ibsen's New Drama." *Fortnightly Review*, LXVII (April, 1900), 575-590.

"The Day of the Rabblement." F. J. C. Skeffington and James A. Joyce, *Two Essays*. Dublin: Gerrard Bros., 1901.

The Holy Office. Pola: Privately printed, 1905.

[In addition to the three items listed above, a number of early essays and reviews have survived; for the texts of these early pieces, see *The Critical Writings of James Joyce*, ed. Ellsworth Mason and Richard Ellmann, New York: The Viking Press, 1959.]

Chamber Music. London: Elkin Mathews, 1907.

Gas from a Burner. [Trieste]: Privately printed, 1912.

Dubliners. London: Grant Richards Ltd., 1914.

A Portrait of the Artist as a Young Man. New York: B. W. Huebsch, 1916.

Exiles. London: Grant Richards Ltd., 1918.

Ulysses. Paris: Shakespeare and Co., 1922. Versions of episodes 1-14 appeared serially in *The Little Review*, 1918-20.

Pomes Penyeach. Paris: Shakespeare and Co., 1927.

Anna Livia Plurabelle [FW 196-216]. New York: Crosby Gaige, 1928.

Tales Told of Shem and Shaun [FW 152-59, 282-304, 414-19]. Paris: The Black Sun Press, 1929.

Haveth Childers Everywhere [FW 532-54]. Paris: Henry Babou and Jack Kahane, & New York: The Fountain Press, 1930.

The Mime of Mick Nick and the Maggies [FW 219-59]. The Hague: The Servire Press, 1934.

Collected Poems. New York: The Black Sun Press, 1936.

Storiella As She Is Syung [FW 260-75, 304-8]. London: Corvinus Press, 1937.

Finnegans Wake. London: Faber & Faber, 1939. In addition to the book publications listed above, fragments of Joyce's *Work in Progress* appeared in several periodicals between 1924 and 1938.

Stephen Hero. Ed. Theodore Spencer. New York: New Directions, 1944. A new edition was issued in 1963, including additional manuscript pages edited by John J. Slocum and Herbert Cahoon.

Letters of James Joyce. Ed. Stuart Gilbert. New York: The Viking Press, 1957. Two additional volumes of letters, edited by Richard Ellmann, have been announced for publication in 1966.

The Critical Writings of James Joyce. Ed. Ellsworth Mason and Richard Ellmann. New York: The Viking Press, 1959. Includes the early essays and reviews, the Paris and Pola notebooks, later political articles, and the broadsides (*The Holy Office* and *Gas from a Burner*).

The Workshop of Daedalus. Ed. Robert Scholes and Richard M. Kain. Evanston: Northwestern University Press, 1965. Contains important manuscript material, including all the extant epiphanies and the 1904 autobiographical fragment, "A Portrait of the Artist."

Giacomo Joyce. Ed. Richard Ellmann. New York: The Viking Press, 1968. A brief manuscript completed before 1915 in which Joyce, in the manner of the epiphanies, broods upon vanished youth and the experience of being infatuated with a young girl. Parts of the work were published in Ellmann's *James Joyce.*

Secondary Sources

I Important Biographical Sources

BUDGEN, FRANK. *James Joyce and the Making of 'Ulysses.'* London: Grayson, 1934; New Ed. Bloomington: Indiana University Press, 1960. An invaluable account of Joyce's attitudes at the time when *Ulysses* was nearing completion (1918-21). Budgen was an intimate friend during the Zurich period.

COLUM, MARY and PADRAIC COLUM. *Our Friend James Joyce.* New York: Doubleday & Co., 1958.
Reminiscences by two lifelong friends.

CURRAN, C. P. *James Joyce Remembered.* New York: Oxford University Press, 1968. Constantine Curran, one of Joyce's close friends at University College, records with fairness and sympathy the events which led up to Joyce's departure from Dublin. Curran is especially good on Joyce's social behavior, his reading, and the intellectual influences which shaped his early life.

ELLMANN, RICHARD. *James Joyce.* New York: Oxford University Press, 1959. The standard biography, an exhaustive and intelligent synthesis of published and unpublished sources. The treatment of Joyce's early life is particularly illuminating.

JOYCE, STANISLAUS. *My Brother's Keeper.* New York: The Viking Press, 1958.

————. *The Dublin Diary of Stanislaus Joyce.* Ed. George H. Healey. Ithaca: Cornell University Press, 1962.

Joyce as seen by his brilliant and exasperating brother. Taken together these two works cover the first twenty-three years of Joyce's life.

SULLIVAN, KEVIN. *Joyce among the Jesuits.* New York: Columbia University Press, 1958.

This account of Joyce's education at Clongowes Wood, Belvedere, and University College illuminates the complex relationship between Stephen Dedalus and his creator. By defining Joyce's actual attitude toward the Jesuits, Sullivan has helped us to understand the ways in which Joyce transformed autobiographical materials.

II Criticism

The critical literature on James Joyce has reached appalling proportions, and each year adds a number of important new studies. I have limited this section of the Bibliography to a listing of significant general studies, followed by a highly selective summary of the ·important criticism on individual works. Inevitably, many useful studies have been omitted, and the student who seeks further information should consult one of the following checklists:

BEEBE, MAURICE, with PHILLIP F. HERRING and WALTON LITZ. "Criticism of James Joyce: A Selected Checklist," *Modern Fiction Studies,* XV (1969), 105-182. The criticism is listed under general headings, and cross-indexed for each of Joyce's works.

DEMING, ROBERT H. *A Bibliography of James Joyce Studies.* Lawrence: University of Kansas Libraries, 1964.

A General Studies

ADAMS, ROBERT M. *James Joyce: Common Sense and Beyond.* New York: Random House, 1966. A balanced survey of the major works, especially good on *Dubliners.*

GIVENS, SEON, ed. *James Joyce: Two Decades of Criticism.* New York: Vanguard Press, 1948, 1963. A collection of important essays from the 1923-48 period.

GOLDBERG, S. L. *James Joyce.* New York: Grove Press, 1962. A brief but suggestive survey of Joyce's total achievement.

GOLDMAN, ARNOLD. *The Joyce Paradox.* Evanston: Northwestern University Press, 1966. An interesting attempt to reconcile some of the divergent critical approaches to Joyce's art. By rehearsing the often conflicting views of Joyce's major critics, Goldman sharpens our sense of the fundamental problems confronted by any reader of Joyce's work. The survey and synthesis does not extend to *Finnegans Wake*

GROSS, JOHN. *James Joyce.* New York: The Viking Press, 1970. A brief, sensitive analysis of Joyce's literary career.

James Joyce Quarterly (The University of Tulsa, 1963-   ). Publishes articles of a rather specialized nature. Especially valuable for its reviews of current criticism.

KENNER, HUGH. *Dublin's Joyce.* Bloomington: Indiana University Press, 1956. An extended analysis of all the works; crotchety but full of brilliant insights.

LEVIN, HARRY. *James Joyce: A Critical Introduction.* Norfolk: New Directions, 1941; Revised Ed. Norfolk: New Directions, 1960. Still one of the best introductions to Joyce's art. Levin emphasizes Joyce's place in the European literary tradition.

MAGALANER, MARVIN, and RICHARD KAIN. *Joyce: The Man, the Work, the Reputation.* New York: New York University Press, 1956. A panoramic study which examines Joyce's life, presents interpretations of the individual works, and charts the progress of Joyce's reputation. Particularly useful for its summaries of critical trends and opinions. Annotated bibliography.

MORSE, J. MITCHELL. *The Sympathetic Alien.* New York: New York University Press, 1959. A series of essays on Joyce and Catholicism.

NOON, WILLIAM. *Joyce and Aquinas.* New Haven: Yale University Press, 1957. The religious aspects of Joyce's art examined from a Catholic viewpoint.

TINDALL, WILLIAM YORK. *James Joyce: His Way of Interpreting the Modern World.* New York: Charles Scribner's Sons, 1950. A broad study which stresses the symbolic unity of Joyce's work.

————. *A Reader's Guide to James Joyce.* New York: The Noonday Press, 1959. Close analyses of each work, designed for the general reader.

WILSON, EDMUND. "James Joyce." *Axel's Castle: A Study in the Imaginative Literature of 1870-1930.* New York: Charles Scribner's Sons,

1931. A pioneering study of Joyce's place in modern literature; Wilson's opinions profoundly influenced the course of subsequent criticism.

B Studies of Individual Works

These special studies should be used in conjunction with the analyses of individual works contained in the General Studies listed above.

1. Poetry
   BAKER, JAMES R. "Joyce's *Chamber Music*: The Exile of the Heart," *The Arizona Quarterly*, XV (Winter, 1959), 349-56. Examines the general themes and structure of *Chamber Music*.
   TINDALL, WILLIAM YORK, ed. *Chamber Music*. New York: Columbia University Press, 1954. A critical edition, with elaborate annotation and commentary. Tindall's scatological reading of the poems should be heavily discounted.
   ZABEL, MORTON D. "The Lyrics of James Joyce," *Poetry*, XXXVI (July, 1930), 206-13. Perceptive, balanced criticism.

2. *Dubliners*
   BRANDABUR, EDWARD. *A Scrupulous Meanness*. Urbana: University of Illinois Press, 1971. A psychoanalytic approach to the stories. Contains final chapters on *Exiles* and *Portrait*.
   GARRETT, PETER K., ed. *Twentieth Century Interpretations of 'Dubliners'*. Englewood Cliffs, N.J.: Prentice-Hall, 1968. A collection of important critical essays.
   GHISELIN, BREWSTER. "The Unity of Joyce's *Dubliners*," *Accent*, XVI (Spring, 1956), 75-88, and (Summer, 1956), 196-213. A pioneering commentary on the symbolic and structural unity of the collection. Reprinted in Garrett, and in Litz and Scholes.
   HART, CLIVE, ed. *James Joyce's 'Dubliners': Critical Essays*. New York: The Viking Press, 1969. Fifteen original essays, one on each story.
   LITZ, A. WALTON, and ROBERT SCHOLES, eds. *Dubliners: Text, Criticism, and Notes*. New York: The Viking Press, 1969. Contains the definitive text, elaborate annotation, bibliography, extracts from the letters, notes on Joyce's revisions, and a collection of critical essays.
   MAGALANER, MARVIN. *Time of Apprenticeship: The Fiction of Young James Joyce*. New York: Abelard-Schuman, 1959. Detailed analysis of the stories, including an examination of earlier drafts.

3. *Stephen Hero*

PRESCOTT, JOSEPH. "James Joyce's *Stephen Hero*," *Journal of English and Germanic Philology*, LIII (April, 1954), 214-23. Relates *Stephen Hero* to the other works.

SPENCER, THEODORE. Introduction to his edition of *Stephen Hero*. New Edition. Norfolk: New Directions, 1963. Still the best general introduction to the work.

4. *A Portrait of the Artist as a Young Man*

ANDERSON, CHESTER G., ed. *A Portrait of the Artist as a Young Man: Text, Criticism, and Notes*. New York: The Viking Press, 1968. Contains the definitive text, elaborate annotation, a gathering of background materials, and a collection of important critical essays. Selected bibliography.

KENNER, HUGH. "The *Portrait* in Perspective." Reprinted in Givens, *Two Decades of Criticism*, and in Anderson. The classic study of theme and structure in the novel.

MAGALANER, MARVIN. *Time of Apprenticeship: The Fiction of Young James Joyce*. New York: Abelard-Schuman, 1959. Considers *Portrait* in the perspective of the early works.

VAN GHENT, DOROTHY. *The English Novel: Form and Function*. New York: Rinehart, 1953. A perceptive reading of the novel's language and symbolism.

Most of the relevant material on *Portrait* has been made readily available by the publication of two anthologies containing criticism and background information.

CONNOLLY, THOMAS E., ed. *Joyce's 'Portrait': Criticisms and Critiques*. New York: Appleton-Century-Crofts, 1962. A collection of essays on *Portrait* and on the esthetic theory; includes the studies by Anderson, Kenner, and Van Ghent. Selective bibliography.

MORRIS, WILLIAM E., and CLIFFORD A. NAULT, eds. *Portraits of an Artist*. New York: The Odyssey Press, 1962. Contains more background information than the Connolly anthology; includes the essays by Anderson, Kenner, Magalaner, and Van Ghent. Also a One-Hundred Item Checklist of publications relevant to *Portrait*.

In *The Workshop of Daedalus* (Evanston: Northwestern University Press, 1965) Robert Scholes and Richard M. Kain have provided the reader of *Portrait* with an invaluable handbook. They have edited all the relevant manuscript materials and have reproduced a number of documents which illuminate the novel's biographical background and its artistic *milieu*. When read in conjunction with *Stephen Hero, The Workshop of Daedalus* provides a step-by-step initiation into the world of Joyce's great autobiographical novel.

5. *Exiles*

ADAMS, ROBERT M. "Light on Joyce's *Exiles?* A New MS, a Curious Analogue, and Some Speculations," *Studies in Bibliography* (Papers of the Bibliographical Society of the University of Virginia), XVII (1964), 83-105. Professor Adams prints the fragments of MS dialogue (mostly from Act III) now held by the Cornell University Library, and speculates upon the literary and biographical significance of this material. The Cornell fragments appear to represent a "private" version of the play.

AITKEN, D. J. F. "Dramatic Archetypes in Joyce's *Exiles*," *Modern Fiction Studies,* IV (Spring, 1958), 42-52.

COLUM, PADRAIC, ed. *Exiles.* New York: The Viking Press, 1951. An edition which prints Joyce's working notes.

FERGUSSON, FRANCIS. "*Exiles* and Ibsen's Work," *Hound and Horn,* V (April-June, 1932), 345-53.

————. "A Reading of *Exiles*," in *Exiles.* Norfolk: New Directions, 1945, pp. v-xviii. Appreciations of the play's dramatic qualities.

6. *Ulysses*

ADAMS, ROBERT M. *Surface and Symbol: The Consistency of James Joyce's 'Ulysses.'* New York: Oxford University Press, 1962. By examining Joyce's transformations of the novel's raw materials, Adams is able to draw useful distinctions between the naturalistic "surface" and the guiding "symbols."

BLACKMUR, R. P. "The Jew in Search of a Son," *Virginia Quarterly Review,* XXIV (Winter, 1948), 96-116. A brilliant study of the cultural forces at play in *Ulysses.* Reprinted in *Eleven Essays in the European Novel* (New York: Harcourt, Brace, 1964).

BLAMIRES, HARRY. *The Bloomsday Book.* London: Methuen & Co., 1966. An intelligent chapter-by-chapter guide and paraphrase.

BUDGEN, FRANK. *James Joyce and the Making of 'Ulysses.'* New Ed. Bloomington: Indiana University Press, 1960. A sympathetic yet objective view of the novel's essential aims. The best introduction to the mind which created *Ulysses.*

CROSS, RICHARD K. *Flaubert and Joyce: The Rite of Fiction.* Princeton: Princeton University Press, 1971. Although it contains chapters on *Dubliners* and *Portrait,* this study is most penetrating on the relations between *Ulysses* and Flaubert's fiction.

ELIOT, T. S. *"Ulysses,* Order, and Myth." Givens, *Two Decades of Criticism.* This early (1923) assessment of the uses of myth in *Ulysses* set the direction for much subsequent criticism. The essay reveals as much about Eliot's intent in *The Waste Land* as it does about Joyce's accomplishment in *Ulysses.*

ELLMANN, RICHARD. *Ulysses on the Liffey.* New York: Oxford University Press, 1972. A detailed, humanistic reading of the novel, based upon the symmetries and correspondences indicated in Joyce's *schema.*

GILBERT, STUART. *James Joyce's 'Ulysses.'* Revised Ed. London: Faber & Faber, 1952. This early (1930) study of the novel's symbolism was written with Joyce's help, but it should not be taken as an authoritative study. Gilbert's emphasis on a rather mechanical symbolism was deliberately conceived as an antidote to those early commentaries which insisted upon the novel's "chaotic" nature.

GOLDBERG, S. L. *The Classical Temper.* London: Chatto and Windus, 1961. The best full-length study of *Ulysses.*

HANLEY, MILES L., ed. *Word Index to James Joyce's 'Ulysses.'* Madison: University of Wisconsin Press, 1937, 1951. A concordance which is of great value to any student of the novel's language and imagery.

HART, CLIVE. *James Joyce's 'Ulysses'.* Sydney: University of Sydney Press, 1968. An intelligent chapter-by-chapter reading of the novel. Contains a fine analytic survey of criticism of *Ulysses.*

KAIN, RICHARD M. *Fabulous Voyager.* Chicago: University of Chicago Press, 1947. Revised Ed. New York: The Viking Press, 1959. An early study of the novel's themes and construction which emphasizes Joyce's use of realistic details.

KLEIN, A. M. "The Black Panther," *Accent,* X (Spring, 1950), 139-155.

————. "The Oxen of the Sun," *Here and Now,* I (January, 1949) 28-48. These ingenious and perceptive studies of the motifs in episodes 1 and 14 represent one extreme in the criticism of *Ulysses;* they should be balanced against the works of Adams and Goldberg.

LITZ, A. WALTON. *The Art of James Joyce: Method and Design in 'Ulysses' and 'Finnegans Wake.'* London: Oxford University Press, 1961, 1964. Analysis of Joyce's shifting artistic ideals as displayed in his methods of composition.

POUND, EZRA. "James Joyce et Pécuchet." Trans. F. Bornhauser. *Shenandoah,* III (Autumn, 1952), 9-20. An early (1922) appreciation stressing the comic and satiric aspects of *Ulysses.*

SCHUTTE, WILLIAM J. *Joyce and Shakespeare*: *A Study in the Meaning of 'Ulysses.'* New Haven: Yale University Press, 1957. A detailed analysis of the Shakespearean motifs, particularly as they relate to the personality of Stephen Dedalus. Contains a comprehensive listing of Shakespeare quotations in *Ulysses.*

STANFORD, W. B. *The Ulysses Theme*: *A Study in the Adaptability of a Traditional Hero.* Oxford: Basil Blackwell, 1954. Useful both for the section on Joyce's *Ulysses* and for the general survey of the Ulysses theme in Western literature.

SULTAN, STANLEY. *The Argument of 'Ulysses.'* Columbus: Ohio State University Press, 1965. A comprehensive analysis based on the narrative action of the novel.

THORNTON, WELDON. *Allusions in 'Ulysses.'* Chapel Hill: University of North Carolina Press, 1968. Detailed annotations of Joyce's more direct references to literature, philosophy, and history. The annotations are cross-referenced and keyed to both the old and new Random House editions.

7. *Finnegans Wake*

ATHERTON, J. S. *The Books at the Wake.* New York: The Viking Press, 1960. A study of literary sources and allusions which illuminates many aspects of structure and meaning.

CAMPBELL, JOSEPH and HENRY MORTON ROBINSON. *A Skeleton Key to 'Finnegans Wake.'* New York: Harcourt, Brace and Co., 1944. An attempt to summarize "what happens" in *Finnegans Wake.* The authors of this pioneer study often distorted and oversimplified the text, but the *Skeleton Key* remains a useful guide. It should be checked against more recent criticism, especially Hart and Glasheen.

GLASHEEN, ADALINE. *A Second Census of 'Finnegans Wake.'* Evanston: Northwestern University Press, 1963. This revised and augmented version of Mrs. Glasheen's original *Census* (1956) is an essential handbook. It contains a detailed synopsis of the *Wake*; a table of "character" transformations; and a census of proper names with page references and extensive commentary.

HART, CLIVE. *Structure and Motif in 'Finnegans Wake.'* London: Faber & Faber, 1962. The best study to date of the *Wake's* design and correspondences; should be used in conjunction with Mrs. Glasheen's *Second Census.*

————. *A Concordance to 'Finnegans Wake.'* Minneapolis: University of Minnesota Press, 1963. This monumental work contains an index to all the "words" in *Finnegans Wake*; a list of the important words and syllables within the compound units;

and a catalogue of "overtones," i.e., English words suggested by Joyce's portmanteau creations.

HAYMAN, DAVID. *A First-Draft Version of 'Finnegans Wake.'* Austin: University of Texas Press, 1963. A transcription of the earliest versions of each episode, based upon a study of the *Finnegans Wake* manuscripts now in the British Museum.

HIGGINSON, FRED H. *Anna Livia Plurabelle: The Making of a Chapter.* Minneapolis: University of Minnesota Press, 1960. Records each stage in the evolution of this complex episode (FW I. viii). Those who wish to understand how the language of *Finnegans Wake* developed out of that of *Ulysses* should consult the editions of Hayman and Higginson.

LITZ, A. WALTON. *The Art of James Joyce: Method and Design in 'Ulysses' and 'Finnegans Wake.'* Revised Ed. New York: Oxford University Press, 1964. Contains a survey of Joyce's work on *Finnegans Wake* and critical commentary based upon the revisions.

A Wake Newslitter (English Dept., University of Dundee, Dundee, Scotland; March 1962-   ). A bi-monthly publication devoted to notes and queries on *Finnegans Wake.*

Index

Index

Swedenborg, Emanuel, 116

Tindall, W. Y., 75
transition, 12
"Two Gallants," 47, 48

Ulysses, 11, 12, 30, 48, 60, 72, 76, 77-98, 99, 100, 102, 109, *115-117;* survey of characters, structure, themes, and language, 78-84; the "Isle of Man" motif, 85-88; the Homeric background, 89-98; Joyce's *schema*, 97.

University College, 9, 22, 23, 24, 26, 27, 29, 30, 66, 73

Verlaine, Paul, 33
Vico, Giambattista, 102-3, 104, 105

Waste Land, The, 67, 68, 77, 80, 100
Woolf, Virginia, 82
Work in Progress, see *Finnegans Wake*

Yeats, William Butler, 9, 10, 20, 21, 22, 23, 25